ANGEL TRACKS in the HIMALAYAS
and
other short stories

by

Gary Shepherd

Khadak Bahadur Lungeli

(April 5, 1912 - November 12, 1996)

DEDICATED

To the memory of

Khadak Bahadur Lungeli and the people of Nepal

Mr. Lungeli, affectionately called "Baju" (Grandfather) by our family, was one of the worst of sinners and one of the finest of saints. Baju became a father to me and a grandfather to my children. By his example, he showed us how to trust God, serve others, and forgive one's enemies. He was kind, caring, and faithful to all. From 1973 to 1991, he patiently taught me the complexities of the Magar language and the intricacies of their admirable culture. He is just one of a multitude of people in Nepal who are very dear to me and my family.

Gary Shepherd
January 2009

PREFACE

To maintain the privacy of certain individuals, the names of some people and places have been changed.

I am grateful to Peter Schmideche, Steve VanRooy, Ron Krueger, Alice Brown and Julie Wilson, for offering their valuable suggestions on the manuscript.

Above all, I am most thankful for my wife, Kerry, who has been so patient with me through the years. She has always encouraged me and has endured wonderfully through the long preparation of this manuscript. She listened and read through my stories a number of times, offering many good ideas to more accurately portray the contents.

My sincere thanks are offered to the Magar people for sharing their lives with me and my family. Apologies are offered where lapse of memory on my part may be responsible for any misrepresentation of fact.

CONTENTS

INTRODUCTION

❧❦❧

This book contains a collection of true stories. In the following pages you will encounter angels and demons, sickness and healing, tragedy and triumph. These stories were written at the request of our daughter, Adina. She wanted a record for her children, so that they would *"Remember how the Lord your God led you all the way,"* (Deuteronomy 8:2).

I grew up on Whidbey Island in Washington State, not far from the Canadian border. We lived in the small rural town of Oak Harbor where my father was a businessman and my mother a school teacher. My life revolved around sports and outdoor activities, particularly hunting and fishing. For many years the Boy Scouts, in which I earned the Eagle Scout award, formed an important part of my life. In 1963, I graduated from the University of Washington with a degree in business and simultaneously, I joined the U.S. Navy as an officer through the ROTC program. There on my ship I began to read the Bible for the first time. After sixteen months of searching, I was led to devote my life to Jesus and to follow His ways for the rest of my life.

My first wife, Barbara, grew up in La Mesa, a suburb of San Diego, California. She graduated at the top of her class from San Diego State University with a degree in education. She was a first grade school teacher who also excelled in music. She participated wholeheartedly in our adventures in Nepal until her tragic death in 1991.

Our daughter, Adina, was born in Nepal in 1971. She and her brother, Michael, who was born in 1973, grew up among the Magar tribal people. Both of them became native speakers of the Magar and Nepali languages. Adina is now a pastor's wife living in Abilene, Texas. Among many other things, she has been involved in grief counseling. Michael is a senior engineer for Dell, Inc. His responsibilities include a focus on memory chip development. He lives with his family in Round Rock, Texas.

My wife, Kerry, is from Melbourne, Australia. I met her in Kathmandu, Nepal, after Barbara's death. She had been working for a number of years as a missionary nurse in various parts of the country.

Nepal is a long and narrow, mountainous country stretching out for 660 miles along the Himalayas. It is sandwiched between India on the south and the Tibetan Plateau on the north. An ancient people called Magars live in the rugged mountains between the mighty Himalayas and the Indian plains. Some tribes have oral histories which tell of their wanderings and settlement in Nepal. The Magars, however, have been in Nepal for so long that I was unable to find anyone who could relate such stories. This leads me to believe that they were among the original settlers of the land.

One of the difficult things I had to deal with while living in a Magar village was the consternation our neighbors experienced when they tried to figure us out. In village life, everyone has a job and position in society. Everyone has an agenda, in particular, one which maintains or improves their social and financial status. What was ours? It wasn't apparent to them at all. We owned no land on which to plant corn, and we had no pigs or goats to raise. Living among the Magar people and just learning their language and culture made no sense to them. How were we planning to get rich from it all?

Over the years I sometimes became frustrated at their persistent probing. One day I let it slip out to an inquirer, "My friend has a secret formula. He can refine gold from monkey tails!"

The secret was out and it spread across the mountains like wildfire. Now they were satisfied. They knew how we would get rich and why we had come. However, my best friend and the village leader, Jipan, understood it was a joke and told some of them so. Nevertheless, this seemed to put an end to their questioning.

Our Magar friends, of course, had no way to understand that someone would actually care to serve the poor and downtrodden, just because they wanted to follow the example of Jesus. Their confusion was further complicated by our attempts to be a model of Jesus' teaching. That is, our primary means

of teaching was by example. If we had come saying
we were teachers, they would have expected that we
would do so more explicitly. We wanted to become
a part of the village fabric though, and let our lives
show them an alternative way of life.

When God created us in His image, one of the
main attributes He gave to mankind was the gift
of a free will. We tried our best to do nothing that
infringed upon that gift of God. If the Magars were to
make changes personally, or in their village society,
we certainly did not want it to come because of false
hope for financial gain or any kind of pressure from
us.

Our friends, and particularly our children's
friends, were frequently dying from one disease or
another. We could and did help the villagers to overcome that. Often, if not annually, there was a severe
food shortage, and sometimes outright famine. We
could and did help them to significantly produce
more food. But the great spiritual oppression they
lived under was another thing.

For about one hundred and fifty years the British
Empire has recruited soldiers from the mountains
of Nepal. Their experience was that the finest came
from four tribes: the Magar, Gurung, Rai and Limbu.
These men were the strongest of the strong, the
faithful of the faithful, and the bravest of the brave.
Consequently, it seemed to be a contradiction that
back in their own villages some of these brave men
would be so fearful of the dark spirit forces. In fact,
the Magars lived in great spiritual bondage which
affected all areas of their lives.

If their crushing spiritual oppression were broken, they might be open to changing the ways that resulted in such poverty and poor health. Our method of teaching was to model with our lives rather than with words. If someone asked us why, unlike themselves, we did not expend huge amounts of money constantly sacrificing to the spirits, then we would explain. But rather than establishing mere religious doctrine, we wanted them to discover for themselves a friendship with Jesus. Therefore, one of our goals was to translate the New Testament into the Magar language. Then, they themselves could make up their own minds regarding what Jesus taught, and they would be free to apply it in ways that best fit their culture.

The stories herein are generally in chronological order. They begin with our early years in Nepal and end with the incidents associated with Barbara's death. A second book following on from this point is anticipated.

For almost forty years, my family and I have been involved with the wonderful Magar people. Our family feels truly fortunate to have lived side by side with some amazing people. Though appearing to be nothing more than backward peasants, some of them deserve to take a stand beside the real heroes of our day.

May those who read these stories be encouraged to trust in God's power, kindness, and unfailing love to those who truly desire to follow Him. They are offered here as an encouragement for Christians who want to apply the teachings of Jesus to their present life situations.

—The Early Years—

(1969-1973)

CHAPTER 1

ANGEL TRACKS IN THE SNOW

*"Have I not commanded you? Be strong and
courageous. Do not be terrified; do not be
discouraged, for the Lord your God will be
with you wherever you go."*
Joshua 1:9

Turn back! **Turn back!!** Old Sheto, our Tibetan
porter, was not talking directly to us, but his
nonstop mantra mumblings and speeding prayer beads
were speaking volumes. He did not want to descend
into this gorge. This was the *Valley-of-No-Return*!

Yes, it certainly looked as though we were
defeated. We would have to go back the way we
had come, and return home a failure. The snow-
pack beneath our feet had hidden the trail, and we
had dead-ended up against immense cloud-encased
cliffs.

Tibetan porters, Angdrak and Sheto

There was one alternative... if you could call it that. We could descend into a deep, snowy gorge and hope that it would lead us to a pass hidden somewhere up among the clouds. To reach the bottom of that gorge, however, we would have to traverse a slope of loose rock covered with snow and ice. The slope was exceedingly steep and the descent would be difficult, as well as dangerous. If we failed to find the pass 3,000 feet higher up the mountain, we could not return this way. It would be impossible to climb back up this slope.

If, however, we managed to cross the pass, we hoped to find the Kham people—a tribe which my colleague David Watters had heard of, but knew next to nothing about. For the past few days, it had been clouding up every afternoon and raining down in the lower elevations. Here at 15,000 feet, however, the clouds dropped snow. The previous day, the locals had warned us that the snow would be waist deep in the pass. No matter how much we offered, no one was willing to guide us over.

David leading us down into the
Valley-of-No-Return

When we had inquired about an alternative route, they had said that with another ten to fourteen days of hard trekking, we could find an open pass farther west. David and I were physically capable of doing that, but we had told our wives, Barbara and Nancy, that we would be back within a month. That circuitous route would get us home at least three weeks late—if all went well—and certainly create some very stressed-out and unhappy wives.

David's knee had given him spats of serious pain after crossing over to the north side of the Himalayan Range. If we took the alternate route and it acted up again, how much longer would that delay us? But if we backtracked, we might only be five days overdue. Nevertheless, that wasn't the point. The question was, "What is God's plan?"

Looking deep into the bottom of the snowy gorge, David pointed out a set of footprints. They were going in the direction of the pass until thick clouds that hugged the ground hid them from view. Where did this fellow come from?

We had spent the night in a tiny shepherd's hut at the tree-line. There we could see for miles across the alpine meadows. The nearest village was back down the mountain, two hours away. We knew that the villagers would not venture out alone at night, because they were terrified of the demons that regularly appeared to them. For this fellow to have gotten beyond our sight on this treeless landscape, he would have had to have left home in the dead of night. It seemed to us the chance of that happening was almost zero.

Our goal was to find this unknown tribe and to get safely back to Kathmandu. We had not come out here for pleasure or adventure, and our *climbing equipment* consisted of a one-hundred-foot-long nylon cord and two umbrellas. Doubtless, the prudent thing to do would be to turn back. Neither of us had any fat left on our bodies, and we now weighed less than 130 pounds.

We had developed a great deal of stamina, and in these mountains we could hike at good speed for twelve hours with hardly a rest. Surely, we could get back to the Dhorpatan airstrip quicker than we had come.

But what about these footprints in the snow? What if God had sent an angel to lead us, and instead we turned back in fear? Would this begin a pattern for our lives? The next time we faced a dangerous or difficult situation, would we make the safe choice? Would we turn back again?

What was God's plan? Wasn't danger the regular companion of destiny? Who knows? Had we come to this snowy mountain for such a time as this? Like Queen Esther 2,500 years before, could we find the courage to say, *"If I perish, I perish!"* (Esther 4:16).

We had expected to be pressing our limits on this search for the Khams and were daily reading of God's promises to protect and guide us. However, we had not expected it to come to this. What if now... what if God had actually provided these footprints in the snow for us? Could we trust the One who had safely brought us this far also to bring us safely home?

As David and I continued to discuss what to do, Sheto's prayer beads moved like lightning through his fingers. Unlike Sheto, however, neither David nor I were now feeling any fear or anxiety. That was the key. It was as God had promised, *"And the peace of God, which transcends all understanding, will guard your hearts and your minds in Christ Jesus,"* (Philippians 4:7).

All of the world's opportunities had been put behind us. Our single goal was to find a tribe to serve, and to expend ourselves bringing them the Good News of hope and peace. We had committed, we had trusted, and over the years we had seen numerous answers to prayer. We had trusted God's promise that *"it is God who works in you, to will and to act according to His good purpose,"* (Philippians 2:13).

To the best of our ability, we had followed His will. Now it was up to Him to do the doing. Yes, we would descend into that snowy gorge. I doubled the thin rope and tied the four of us together. Then David led us over the steep rim into that Valley-of-No-Return. Today we were rolling the dice for all the chips. Today, we expected to find this lost tribe or die trying!

"Those who hope in Me will not be disappointed."
Isaiah 49:23

—Postscript—

This experience occurred in October 1969. The next day we learned from the villagers of Kisne Village that no one had crossed the pass ahead of us. At that point we began to refer to those footprints as *"Angel Tracks."* Were they really made by a heavenly angel? Or could someone have come ahead of us and then stayed in the forest instead of continuing on into the village? It was possible, but very unlikely. Even more unlikely was the possibility that someone would have made that trip by himself.

Nevertheless, whether the tracks were made by a human or by an angel, on that day they were there for us to follow. Without them, we would have undoubtedly turned back and returned to Kathmandu without finding the Kham villages. For us, those footprints were made by a messenger of God to lead us over that cloud-enshrouded pass and down the treacherously steep face of a Himalaya. For us, they were certainly *"Angel Tracks."*

Shepherd's hut

CHAPTER 2

NO TURNING BACK

Every hair on my body was standing straight up! Peering carefully over the trail's edge, all I could see was empty space and swirling clouds swallowing up the cliff a thousand feet below us.

"How far down is it?" David inquired.

Rather irritated, I thought to myself, "Why does he have to know that?"

This was probably the fourth cliff that we had encountered, and they all seemed about the same. We had been following a very poor semblance of a trail that wound like a maze across the Himalaya's face. Near the tops of these immense cliffs were bridges made of four or five old poles joined together to span fifteen or twenty feet of emptiness. These rough poles seemed hardly thicker than my arms, and as for the weathered grass ropes which lashed them together... they looked old and half-rotten.

Words can't tell you how much I hated to put my feet on those poles. But there was no turning back.

We were committed. Earlier that day, David had led us from the north side of the Himalayas over an 18,000 foot pass on the west shoulder of Sisni Lekh. Most of the way there was no obvious trail. Instead, we were simply following a single set of footprints in the snow. For another couple hours, David followed the tracks that crisscrossed the face of the Himalaya. But now, we had an additional worry. This was the south face and the afternoon sun was melting the snow. So as we continued descending on this precarious and barely-discernable trail, we were finding the imprints less often. If we missed the path, we would not survive for long trying to forge our own way.

I don't remember why I was out in front now... just that I was. For hours, David had led us through some very dangerous places. But nothing was as hair-raising for me as the primitive bridges which hugged the face of these cliffs.

To negotiate each crossing, I turned sideways. Then I stretched my arms out spread-eagle, leaned into the cliff, and put my hands on the cold wet rock. Trying to minimize the strain on those old ropes, I moved my feet slowly and carefully. With each little movement, however, the bridge poles creaked and bent under my weight. Once I crossed the chasm, David would come, then our Tibetan porters, Sheto and Angdrak.

At the first crossing I had looked down, lost my balance, and had almost been sucked over the side head-first. After that, I didn't look down without first putting my hand on the mountain to steady myself... not that there was anything to hold on to. One time

I had gotten down on my hands and knees and had tried to peer over. But by now, I had had my fill of looking. There was really no point in knowing: five hundred feet... one thousand feet... two thousand feet. If one went over the side the result would be the same.

We had eaten breakfast at sunup on the north side of the Himalayas. In order to be fair, I had put the last of our oatmeal, our remaining sugar, two tiny eggs, and a few scraps of old sheep meat into the pot. Mixing it together, I had served out equal-but-skimpy portions of this most un-delicious meal. Just to reach the pass had taken a great deal of energy. Then the zigzag descent down the southern face had been constant high-stress and energy-consuming. Any stumble or misstep could easily be our last. With nothing more to eat, we wondered how we could continue to push on at that altitude without becoming dizzy or shaky. I suppose it was God, adrenalin, or both that kept us steady.

Anyway, I'd really had enough of these bridges and their poles going "ngyaaak, ngyaaak, ngyaaak" every time I shuffled my feet. Why did David have to know how far down it was?! Irritated, I glanced quickly into the abyss and answered, "It doesn't matter! If this goes down, we're going up!"

Today, we were giving God ample opportunity to prove Himself. When we had descended into that first snowy gorge, I had lost my footing on the ice-covered scree and had wrenched my ankle. To my amazement, it didn't seem to bother me much at all. Any injury of consequence on this mountain and it would be all over. One could barely keep his own body on this track, much less carry anyone else out. If one of the bridges took me down, my companions would be stranded. They would have to try to get back over the pass. Then, they would need to find a way out of the Valley-of-No-Return before they froze to death. Yes, God had plenty of opportunity to be God today.

"On that day they will say, 'Surely this is our God; we trusted in Him, and He saved us.'"
Isaiah 25:9

Sisni Lekh in summer time

CHAPTER 3

THE CHICKEN DINNER

The daunting task of crossing row upon row of steep, craggy mountains stared us in the face. Having come over the pass and down the treacherous southern face of Sisni Lekh, we had spent the night in a rocky ravine at the tree line. We awoke hungry the next morning and hiking at a rapid pace arrived about 10 a.m. at Kisne Village. There, David learned from the villagers that people weren't crossing the pass these days and that no one had come ahead of us. It was at this time, we began to call the footprints which we had followed, *"Angel Tracks."*

All the food our hardy Tibetan porters could carry was now gone and we were hungry. These villagers, however, weren't particularly friendly. After much effort David finally managed to purchase a small bowl of tiny potatoes, which we and our two porters quickly devoured.

Looking across the rows of mountains, I calculated we ought to reach the confluence of the Kisne and Uttar Ganga rivers in two days. Even though we were in top physical condition, my assumption was way off. That wretched trail seemed to go every way except forward! It would zigzag along a knife blade-like ridge only to reverse right back around the other side. Then the trail would plummet hundreds of feet down into a dark, cavernous ravine and come straight back up. It was really frustrating. Sometimes we could nearly throw a rock back across to where we had been half an hour earlier. After pushing hard all day we had made very little progress.

In this rugged country, habitation was sparse. When we did come across some villagers, they didn't want to sell us food even though it was harvest time. On the occasions that they did give us something, it would only be a couple of tiny eggs or a handful of potatoes... all to share between four famished men. Being on the trail day after day had given us lots of time to talk. The longer we'd been traveling, the simpler and plainer our diet had become. Over the past two weeks we had sometimes passed the hours by discussing in great detail the kinds of foods not available in Nepal. "Oh, to have a juicy hamburger with mayonnaise, lettuce, and tomatoes!"

After four hard, long days we finally reached the Uttar Ganga, only to find that there was no bridge and that the river was too swift and deep to ford. Backtracking, we came across four lonely huts perched on a steep outcropping. The sun was sinking behind the mountains and by then we were thoroughly exhausted.

As Americans, we were *untouchables* in this Hindu Kingdom, and could never be certain of the reception we would receive. If we were welcomed, we usually expected to stay on a bumpy, outside porch. When we asked one fellow, we were relieved to find that he would accommodate us. Then to our great joy he also agreed to sell us a rooster, six small eggs, a cucumber, and some corn flour! Along with some yoghurt, this went far in renewing our flagging spirits.

The next morning, we braced ourselves against the chill with a quick cup of tea and a boiled egg. Then we started down the trail at 6:30 a.m. and made the long descent to the crossing on the Kisne. At the ford, the icy river ran almost to our waists, so we crossed carrying our clothes above our heads. A little farther on, we came across some herdsmen with their water buffalo. They were happy enough to sell us huge bowls of rich yoghurt. That helped temporarily, but within a couple of hours our stomachs were empty again.

There was no such thing as a straight or flat trail out here. The river bank ran through deep gorges and steep cliffs, and to skirt around them, the trail always wound up or down. Often the mountain was so steep that staircase-like steps had been dug out of the sharp mountainside. Some of these were hundreds and hundreds of feet straight up.

I especially disliked those stairs. First, there was the extra strain of climbing so steeply. But more so, if I slipped, there was nothing to stop me from tumbling clear to the bottom. That could be fatal.

About noon time we took a little rest at the river. There the trail crossed to the south bank of the Uttar Ganga. We had been told that as we moved on up the valley we would find Kham villages. Eventually, this river would take us back to the Dhorpatan airstrip and home.

In the past few days, the hungrier we had become the more our imagination and conversations had run wild about food. Dripping with sweat in the middle of the day, one of us might inquire, "How would a chocolate milkshake taste right now?" Often we would speculate about what our wives, Barbara and Nancy, would cook for us when we got home. There was no doubt in my mind that we would have good red meat to renew our shrinking frames. After thirty tough days on the trail, what kind of steak would Barbara fix for me?

About 4:30 p.m. we finally reached the Kham village of Gharkhani. I was thinking that we could still make it to the next village before dark, but David suddenly sat down and announced, "I'm not going another step further until I get something to eat!"

The village was large and we inquired about staying the night. After a while, we were led to a house where we were greeted royally by a retired Gurkha soldier who had served under British officers. He was thrilled that two Americans—Allies whom he had fought beside in World War II—were visiting his secluded village. What could he get for us?

Off he went, scouring the village. Soon he was back with a few small eggs, some rice and wheat flour. Wow!

Chicken? After a bit he was back with a rooster under each arm. That night and the next morning we most gratefully gorged ourselves. But, to our dismay, we found that our stomachs had shrunk so much that we couldn't eat nearly all that we desired.

About noon the following day, we reached the Kham village of Shera where a lady freely gave us each a plate of honeycomb to eat. We marveled at how different these friendly tribal people were compared to the high-caste people of Kisne Valley. David decided to stay the night in Shera, hoping to make arrangements for his family to come back there to live. Meanwhile, I could push on with our Tibetan porter, Sheto, in order to reach Dhorpatan by the next day. In this way we could get a radio message out for the plane to come pick us up sooner.

Ignoring my feet, which had been sore for the past few days, we set off. As evening came, we found four little houses below the trail. One fellow was particularly friendly. He not only allowed us to stay the night, but also agreed to sell us a chicken. Amazing! In three days we had gotten four chickens. The following day, Sheto and I reached the Tibetan refugee camp in Dhorpatan and the message went out. A day-and-a-half later, Wayne Aeschliman picked us up in a Cessna 206 and flew us back to Kathmandu.

I had gotten used to sleeping on hard, lumpy ground, so the appeal of getting home was not a comfortable bed. But oh, to have a good meal! I couldn't wait to see what Barbara had planned. She was a great cook and how delicious, how satisfying it would be. How I craved to have some familiar food.

41

I was so anxious to eat that meal, but my watch just wouldn't seem to cooperate. The clock hands seemed to move at a crawl! Finally, dinner time arrived and I sat down at the table. Barbara had worked very hard and was obviously pleased with the results of her effort. When she set out that beautiful meal, I couldn't believe my eyes. At the center of it was a roast chicken. I nearly cried. Then I fibbed terribly, telling her how wonderful the meal was.

The chicken dinner, of course, tasted great. It was just that my expectations had been so different. On the trail day after day, our food had become so basic, so skimpy, so very little... and if there was meat, then it was chicken only. Furthermore, for the past couple weeks we had talked about how different it would be when we got home. It had been so foolish of me to let my thoughts run riot over food. We had wasted so many hours, so many days detailing the delights of wonderful American foods. But the fixation was too much.

God knew that I could do more productive things with my mind. In the nearly forty years that have passed since that day, I have never again been tempted to dream about food. I have allowed my mind to become preoccupied with other silly things, but never again with food.

With regards to food, I can say with Paul, *"I have learned to be content whatever the circumstances,"* (Philippians 4:11).

—Postscript—

David and his family returned to Shera. There they learned the Kham language and culture and helped the people with their medical needs and in other practical ways. During the ensuing years they encountered many dangers and great trials, as well as numerous sicknesses which eventually cost Nancy her health. Through it all, the footprints-in-the-snow experience encouraged them to persevere in this remote corner of the Himalayas.

Sixteen years later, a Kham New Testament translation was completed. In an attempt to stop the spread of the Good News during the 1980s and 1990s, the government launched a campaign of terror, imprisonment, and torture for many Kham Christians. This culminated in the extrajudicial execution of two pastors and five elders of the Kham church.

CHAPTER 4

THE CALL

❧❧❧

The place was packed out and we were standing shoulder to shoulder against the back wall of our little church in San Diego, California. Canadian evangelist, Reverend Clarence Shrier, had been preaching a series of powerful messages that week and the meeting was closing with "Amazing Grace," a song I particularly loved.

It was February 1969, and Barbara and I were getting ready to leave the next month for our first five-year stint in Nepal. We had completed our linguistics courses with Wycliffe and had spent nearly six months at Jungle Camp in Southern Mexico. There we had been taught how to live among an ancient people in some remote part of the world. Our financial support was coming together now, and our steel drums were packed for shipment. We had no idea what sort of language or tribe we would encounter, but in that Hindu kingdom where Christians were frequently persecuted, we were certain that God would guide us to the right place at the right time.

I was rejoicing in the powerful teaching and the response it had evoked in the crowd. Just four years earlier, I had dedicated my life to Jesus Christ and these words of "Amazing Grace" were very meaningful. God's mercy to me, one who was once His enemy, never ceased to move me, and I sang the words from my heart. Eventually we came to the last stanza:

"When we've been there 10,000 years,
bright shining as the sun,
We've no less days to sing God's praise
than when we'd first begun."

As we were about to begin, a quiet voice suddenly pierced my heart, "That's so dandy for you to be there for 10,000 years, but what about those who have never heard the Good News?"

This hymn had been written by that sinner of sinners, the slave trader, John Newton. Surely it was proper for him to proclaim this promise of eternal joy. But in that instant my focus was turned to the distant corners of the earth... to those who lived in darkness and hopeless fear. "No," I decided, "I will not sing those lines until we have translated a New Testament for an unknown tribe!"

A month later, Barbara and I left for Nepal. The people were wonderful and friendly, but we knew that sharing about Jesus was not only illegal, it could get us and our friends expelled. In fact, in 1976 false charges were made to the authorities and we were all forced to leave. Nevertheless, six months later Barbara and I returned and continued our work. For the next few years we never thought that it was possible to complete a New Testament translation. The opposition was too great, the obstacles were too huge. Year after year whenever that song was sung, I was silent for the last stanza—my heart pierced again by thoughts of the multitudes around the world living in darkness without hope.

During our first two years of marriage, God had been leading Barbara and me into the work of Wycliffe. But that moment in San Diego secured and sealed for me all that had come before. Now the call to follow came with a deeper certainty, a new intensity, and a determination to never quit. Pull back we would. Rest, yes. Revise our plans, of course. But until God gave us the peace to lay it down, my heart would always be with those living in darkness.

> *"How, then, can they call on the One they have not believed in? And how can they believe in the One of whom they have not heard?"*
> Romans 10:14

—Postscript—

Twenty-two years later the Magar New Testament was dedicated in Dallas. At the dedication ceremony I sang that last stanza once again. But as the years have continued to pass, while there are still an unknown number of people groups who have yet to hear a message of hope, I have failed to find joy in those lines. Perhaps in carrying the light of God's Kingdom into one small dark corner of the earth, I have seen too much suffering and injustice, too much sickness and dying, too much fear and hopelessness.

CHAPTER 5

THEN SINGS MY SOUL
❧❦❧

"the God of glory thunders..."
"The voice of the Lord strikes with
flashes of lightning..."
Psalm 29:3, 7

B arbara and I had been in Nepal for a year, and for the past five months we had been learning the Magar language in Yangchok Village in Tanahu District. It was March 1970. Every other Saturday, we made the two-hour journey along the rising ridge to the bazaar in Bandipur. There we hoped to come across a few eggs and perhaps even some withered, old vegetables in the tiny shops.

On our return that afternoon, we followed a deserted trail along a rugged ridge. To our left the ridge dropped off almost vertically, sometimes uncovering great limestone cliffs. Everywhere birds were singing their joyful springtime songs. A warm breeze was gently rising up the mountain and it bathed us in the strong sweet perfume of the flowering mahogany forest. Thousands of feet below, clear green water that originated in snow banks on the Tibetan border tumbled peacefully over great boulders in the Marsyandi River. And from East to West, as far as our eyes could see, a panorama of snow-covered Himalayas stretched out before us.

Village corn storage and Himalayas

As the day wore on, twenty-five miles to the north, hot humid air rushing up from India collided with the 26,000 foot Himalayas. The resulting uplift produced a small thundercloud which began to grow quickly. Unable to cross the Himalayan Massif, the storm turned angrily eastward. Moving rapidly along the face of the snow fields, wild winds gave birth to a miniature cyclone. Arrows of lightning began flashing forth from its dark boiling midst with an increasing tempo. After some pause, great peals of earth-shaking thunder crashed and then echoed back and forth through the valleys. The sight was most spectacular!

For us, however, all was calm and peaceful. From our perch, we could see the gigantic snow-covered mountains, the River, the furious storm and the staccato fire of lightning. The fragrant warm breeze continued, but the birds had quieted as if in reverence to their Creator. It was a mixture of beauty, fearsome power, and peace like we had never experienced before. Deeply moved by the scene, our hearts recalled that song we had sung not so long ago at our little church in San Diego:

"O Lord my God, when I in awesome wonder,
Consider all the works Thy hands have made.
I see the stars, I hear the rolling thunder,
Thy power throughout the universe displayed.

When through the woods and forest glades I wander,
And hear the birds sing sweetly in the trees;
When I look down from lofty mountain grandeur,
And hear the brook, and feel the gentle breeze.

And when I think that God, His Son not sparing,
sent Him to die I scarce can take it in.
That on the cross my burden gladly bearing,
He bled and died to take away my sin.

Then sings my soul, my Savior God to Thee:
How great Thou art! How great Thou art!"

We felt so small and insignificant on that mountain as we watched that mighty storm move along
the face of the immense Himalayan Range. We were
so alone in that empty forest... but God was so very
close. We were cut off from all that was familiar
and comfortable, but certainly we were not cut off
from God.

"The heavens declare the glory of God;
the skies proclaim the work of His hands."
Psalm 19:1

—Postscript—

We were living now on the other side of the
world and felt so isolated from family and friends.
At that time we were the only followers of Jesus
among the thousands of people in a multitude of
nearby villages. Also, we were sometimes made
to feel so small and degraded as *untouchables* in a
Hindu land.

In 1979, Kerry, my second wife also had a
similar experience. One day she was out on the trail
alone. When she looked out at the grandeur of the

Himalayas and God's creation it was so moving that she spontaneously broke out singing at the top of her voice "How Great Thou Art."

CHAPTER 6

THE AIRSTRIP

Where would we get the extra money? We had been in Nepal for fourteen months, and our income was about $350 a month. Before we left home, 80% of our estimated need had been promised by friends and churches. Wycliffe's experience was that once we arrived overseas the donations would increase. They had been right, but this amount would only cover our regular expenses.

The trek from Palungtar airstrip to Yangchok Village, where we were living, required us to cross the Marsyandi River by dugout canoe. When the flight was delayed, which was often, we couldn't reach the river before dark. In a Hindu land, we Christians had to be careful not to defile someone's home by stepping inside. Consequently, we would spend the night shivering on someone's hard dirt veranda as we fitfully tried to get a little rest.

Major Nar BahadurThapa was the leader in that area and he had invited us to live in his village. In the

British Gurkha forces he had been an engineer, as well as Queen Elizabeth's personal body guard. Now he had found a piece of unused land this side of the river. There we should build an airstrip, he insisted. The window of opportunity was now... in the month of May. The villagers were waiting for the monsoon rains to plant their rice, so they weren't pressed with other work. Major Thapa would rally the villagers, and within a few weeks they would clear the trees and level the rough places, he said.

However, we had no way to inform our supporters quickly and who knows what it would cost. Should we wait until we had the money in hand? If we did, the chance to build the airstrip would be postponed for a year. We could, however, go into debt and hopefully pay it back sometime later. We had gotten this far by pushing our faith to its limits. Should we stop now? A verse that we often remembered in those early days was, *"and my God will supply all your needs according to His riches in Christ Jesus!"* (Phil. 4:19)

Each week we had two small aluminum boxes carrying our mail, one coming and one going, on Royal Nepal Airline's DC-3 from Palungtar. We told Major Thapa to begin the work. Then we wrote to Kathmandu and asked for 2,000 rupees to be sent out the next week.

We knew that our letters from Nepal would take four weeks or more to reach the U.S — if they weren't lost. Practically speaking, it would take a minimum of two-and-a-half months for us to receive the first gifts from any of our supporters who might respond to this extra need.

Work progressed well on the airstrip and near the end of May it was completed. On June 4, 1970, Wayne Aeschliman set the Cessna 206 down on the bumpy one-way strip, braking to a halt just before running into the brush at the foot of a steep forested ridge. He told us the strip was passable, but to make it functional we had to do more work. The larger humps had to be cut down. With nothing but hoes, that would take a lot of time and even more money. Meanwhile, I added up what we had spent so far, and it totaled right at $500. At our level of monthly income, this was a substantial amount of debt.

After the worst of the humps were shaved down, Wayne came back on June 20th. He brought our mail with him, which included our April financial statement from Wycliffe. In addition to their regular amount, Harold and Jody Franz had sent us an extra donation of $500. Then I added up what cutting down the humps had cost. That was another $200. In July we were back in Kathmandu when we received our May statement from Wycliffe. Once again Harold and Jody had sent us an extra amount. It was exactly $200.

"Before they call I will answer..."
Isaiah 65:24

—Postscript—

Harold and Jody had no inkling whatsoever that we were in such dire need of more money. We learned later that they had received some extra income in April and once again in May. In each case, they felt that they should share part of it with us. This experience went a long way in helping us not to worry and to just trust God for our unplanned needs. Yes, we would budget and save as we could. But most of all, we would rest our hearts and minds on our Heavenly Father.

This experience also encouraged us to give generously. We were often in a position to know when friends and colleagues were in crisis and had unexpected financial needs. When we had money available, sometimes we could give substantial amounts. Just as Harold and Jody had blessed us unexpectedly, so too, others were blessed from an unexpected source. After all, we reasoned, we were all a part of God's Kingdom work. So investing in the Kingdom was always a good idea.

CHAPTER 7

THE COOKIE

*"Ask, and you shall receive, that your
joy may be full."*
John 16:24

Full of faith, the little fellow never failed to put in
an appearance when the time was right. Though
he was too shy to ask directly, it was always clear
what was on his heart... and his faith never went
unrewarded.

The house we shared in Kathmandu with the
Watters family was identical upstairs and downstairs. There was a hallway through the middle with
individual rooms off both sides. Barbara and I lived
downstairs, while David and Nancy with their two
little boys lived upstairs. The only access they had to
go outside, however, was to come downstairs, make
a turn at our kitchen, and walk through our hallway
out to the front door.

Stevie, Nancy, Daniel and David Watters

Back in 1970, we were particularly pleased when we received a package of chocolate chips in the mail. Barbara used them very sparingly, and every few weeks she would bake chocolate chip cookies. In doing so, the aroma would waft up the stairs to the Watters' abode. Before long, their oldest son, Stevie, would take it upon himself to pay "Aunt Barbara," as he called her, a visit.

Innocently, this quiet little four-year-old would appear at the top of the stairs, his hands tightly clutching the handrail posts. Pausing between steps, Stevie would make his way slowly down to our kitchen. Inevitably he would inhale deeply and then say, "Ummmm, do I smell something gooood?"

Well, everyone in the house smelled something, and it smelled very good. Everyone knew it wasn't just cookies... it was chocolate chip cookies! Barbara readily understood Stevie's unstated request and she would hand him a cookie. Unhurried then, he would make his way up the stairs, savoring his treasure with great delight.

When Barbara was dropping dough onto the cookie sheet, she always counted on giving one or two to Stevie. She expected him to ask and she loved to fulfill his heart's desire. In doing so, we too received great joy over the big smiles and obvious happiness it brought him.

—Postscript—

God is clear in Genesis, the Book of Beginnings, that He has made us in His likeness. If we love to give the little children pleasure, how much more must He? But all too often, our concept of God has become clouded... has become too small, and we forget.

When we fail to remember that it gives our Father great pleasure to bless His children, we will fail to trust that His loving mercy is new every morning. Then, we can easily forget that His greatest desire is to plan the very best for us.

If our desires are *slow* to be fulfilled and we forget His plan, we will begin to lose patience. And when our prayer is not answered according to our schedule, we may lose our perseverance to trust that God has a bigger plan for us. Then we will face the test: When we can't see His hand, will we still trust His heart?

Stevie, however, knew Barbara's heart, and I never saw him leave her presence disappointed.

A TRIBUTE

On May 18, 2009, my "Angel Tracks" companion was unexpectedly called home to be with the Lord. David E. Watters was 65 years old. I, among others, considered him a friend like no other.

He was a common man with uncommon abilities. He had every opportunity to live a most comfortable life. Instead, he chose to sit with dirt-poor tribal people in lean-tos and huts around smoky fires. Their struggles and problems were always a deep concern for him, and he did all he could to alleviate them.

David completed a PhD in Linguistics at the University of Oregon in 1998 and went on to become known as one of the foremost scholars in the world on the languages of Nepal. For many years he taught in the Central Department of Linguistics at Tribhuvan University, where he was a valuable mentor to scores of Nepalese students.

David had a significant role in the translation of the New Testament into Kham, as well as numerous community development projects. He was recently honored by the Kham Magar nation as their "champion" at a formal ceremony in Kathmandu. Many among the Kham affectionately refer to him as "Grandfather."

I greatly miss his wisdom, joyful spirit, and linguistic knowledge.

CHAPTER 8

THE WITCH

🙙🙚🙙🙚

Shouting out curses, the witch paced back and forth across the school yard. Interestingly, she was careful to remain outside the village, yet close enough for people to hear her. Apparently it would be unacceptable for her to spew out her curses inside the borders of the village itself.

"I've ruined us! I've ruined us!" Barbara moaned. It was dark and she was deeply distressed when I arrived home. We had been trying our best to fit in with the Magar way of doing things, but she had failed badly today. Everyone in the village knew it, too.

I had been gone all day... out hunting on Peak-of-the-gods with some of the men. Meanwhile, Barbara had been at home with our little daughter, carrying on with her regular routine. As usual, large numbers of people had come to visit. Many just liked to see a white person and observe how different we looked and lived. Others needed critical medical help for themselves or for their children. We were not familiar with everyone yet, including one lady who lived on the far side of the gorge. She was short and not unattractive... probably in her early thirties.

It was 1972 and we had moved south from Yangchok Village across the mountains. There, in the inaccessible areas of Palpa District, the Magar language was not being mixed with Nepali. In those mountains, Arakhala Village was the largest of the Magar villages.

Usually, we would plan to stay in Arakhala for two or three months at a time. In that poor out-of-the-way village, very little was available and we didn't like to deprive them by asking to buy what little they did have. Consequently, we packed up all of our necessary food and supplies in one-gallon or five-gallon tins and brought it with us.

Tins, it turned out, were treasured by the villagers, because in those days they had no means to keep the hordes of rats from chewing up or eating their things. So, soon after we arrived, people would begin asking us for empty tins. Of course, none of them were empty right away, so Barbara would write their names on a list. On the last day of our stay, we would distribute the tins to the villagers. Back then they had precious little money, so we refused to put a price on them or sell them. Instead, we let them give us whatever extra they had, whenever they had it. Sometimes, with false hopes of moving their names to the top of the list to secure a tin, our friends would bring us a couple of eggs, some vegetables, or something else as a gift beforehand.

It was getting to the end of our stay now, and Barbara's list was already longer than the number of tins we would have available. When Shami came in, she asked for one. Barbara explained that they had all been spoken for. Shami, however, wouldn't accept that. Instead, she pointed to a large tin and said, "Give me that one!"

Barbara declined. Then Shami pointed to another and declared, "Well then, give me that one!"

Barbara reiterated that none were available. It didn't matter to Shami, however, and she demanded this one, then that one, then another. Barbara became confused by this aggressive behavior. She didn't know what else to do other than continue to explain that she didn't have any... they were all spoken for. Finally, Shami left in a huff.

A few minutes later, Barbara heard what sounded like shrieks coming from the empty school yard. It was Shami, and she was yelling something or other which included Barbara's name. Barbara was shaken and didn't know how she could have done anything different. In any event, she reckoned that she had not only made Shami our enemy, but probably everyone else who was related to her.

When I heard the story, I wasn't too concerned and reassured her that she had done the right thing. The Magars are extremely polite and rather shy about asking. And for sure, I had never heard of one of them demanding something, so I was certain that Shami's behavior was not within the cultural norm. Still, we had a lot to learn about Magar culture, and this was so far out of the norm that I was suspicious

Shami might even be a witch. I told Barbara not to worry about it. I would talk with Jipan, the village leader, and if we needed to do anything to restore the situation, then we would do it.

The next day I told Jipan the story and he assured me not to be concerned. She was just like that, he said. It took us a long time to build the confidence and friendships necessary to learn some of the village secrets, and it wasn't easy to discover what the real deal was. I don't remember for sure, but I suppose it was Jipan who affirmed my suspicions some days later that she was a witch.

I wasn't the least surprised. Witches can break the cultural rules because they live outside them. She, in particular, was said to have powerful familiar spirits doing her bidding. No one dared to stand in her way. If she asked for something, she was immediately appeased. But poor Barbara didn't know this. She didn't know that no one ever said "no" to Shami! She didn't know that when Shami asked, one was supposed to be petrified.

The next time we came to Arakhala, Shami came by our house again. She was cheery and acted as if nothing whatsoever had ever happened. Barbara wrote her name down on the list, and before we left the village we made sure to send her a tin with someone who was going over to Peak-of-the-gods.

—Postscript—

In the coming years, Baju helped us enormously in understanding Magar ways and learning village secrets. One thing we were told was that witches like Shami did not live for long. The very spirits who worked for her would bring her to an early end. And, in fact, one time we came back to Arakhala and learned that she had died rather suddenly... and apparently to no one's sorrow.

Witches and witchdoctors need to be careful when they send forth their familiar spirits on a mission. If those spirits cannot carry out their assigned deed and become overly frustrated, they may return and inflict that very curse upon their host. I often wondered if this could have been what happened to Shami.

"The trouble he causes recoils on him;
his violence comes down on his own head."
Psalm 7:16

"Let the wicked fall into their own nets,
while I pass by in safety."
Psalm 141:10

Arakhala Village — 1972

CHAPTER 9

THE CURSE

❧❧❧

What was that rustling the leaves? What was sneaking up behind me?

Somehow I managed to maintain my tenuous perch on the mountainside and turn without making a noise. Carefully, I scanned the bushes and bamboo thickets below. From this very location Baju had shot and killed a Bengal tiger. Though tigers seldom came this way any more, there were still plenty of leopards and bears around.

There it was again! Momentarily, something had stirred the dry leaves... and then all was quiet. Finally, I caught a glimpse of a shadowy form making its way stealthily through the thick undergrowth.

We hadn't been living in Arakhala Village for long, and this was probably the third time that the village men had asked me to go hunting with them. Baju had come along, too, eager as ever. Even though he was over sixty years old and had only one leg, when we climbed those steep ridges on Peak-of-the-gods, it always took all of my energy just to keep up with him.

Leaving for the hunt

Baju had grown up on this mountain and he knew every nook and cranny by name. On this day, he had led me to a place that was a natural funnel and shown me where to expect the game to emerge. The tree behind which I was instructed to hide was the very one from which he had shot two wild boar and a tiger with his old muzzle loader. That, however, was many years ago and now the brush had grown so thick that I could only see ten or fifteen feet in front of me. From there an animal would be able to reach me in a single bound! This was not to my liking, so as soon as Baju left, I moved twenty feet down the back side of the steep ridge.

Three or four men with their ancient muzzle loaders, and I with my little .22 rifle had been placed at the favorite ambush spots on the ridgeline. The others had gone down the mountain about a mile and had started a drive back up through the deep virgin forest. Throwing rocks, beating sticks and coughing, they hoped to push the animals up to us. The first time I went out with them, I heard the sporadic blasts from their guns and thought for sure that we would have lots of meat.

I soon learned, however, that their guns were so inaccurate that eight or ten shots and no meat was the standard for this sort of hunt. In fact, from time to time, it was seriously stated that they would be more successful if they went back to shooting bows with poison-tipped arrows like their grandfathers had done. So it had been that day... a shot here, a shot there. Nothing, however, had come my way until now. But what was the deal? This animal was coming up from behind me. He was going towards the beaters, not away!

Then suddenly a barking deer appeared across the ravine about 40 yards away. He was standing at the edge of a patch of *ninggala* bamboo. I had hoped for a closer shot, but this would be my only chance. When I squeezed the trigger he spun around and crashed back down the mountain. Then all was quiet. About half an hour later the drive was over and Jipan came to get me. He was thrilled when I told him I had shot a deer. But when he went to assemble

71

the other hunters to help him find it, they wouldn't budge. How could such a tiny gun kill a deer at such a great distance? Either I was trying to fool them, they thought, or else I was telling a boastful story!

I didn't want to lose my mark of where the deer had been standing, so I had not moved since I had fired. Jipan and Sailha alone believed me. When they reached the bamboo patch, I guided them in the direction that the deer had gone. Slowly and methodically they followed the tracks. When they had gone about thirty feet Jipan called out excitedly, "There's blood! He's hit! Hurry! Get down the mountain! Get ahead of the wounded animal!"

But no one moved. Not a man.

I wondered about their inaction, but this was the first time I had been with them when an animal had been hit and I didn't know what was normal. Five minutes later, however, everything changed when Sailha yelled out, "He's here! He's here!" Suddenly the hunters bolted. Within a few minutes they had carried the deer to the top of the ridge. Men who had been exhausted by the heat of the day and the exertion of the hunt were suddenly full of exhilaration and excitement. I was rather puzzled as I watched them. They seemed to be almost drunk with joy.

That evening, we were still on the mountain when they began cutting up the barking deer. The custom, they had often told me, was that the person who shot an animal would receive the two hind quarters. The remainder of the animal would be divided evenly among the other hunters. But while they were processing the deer, one of the hunters came and asked me for permission to change their hunting custom. Because the bulk of the meat was in the hind quarters, the rest of the men would receive only a very small portion. If they themselves were ever lucky enough to shoot an animal, they would never agree to a reduction of their share... the meat was far too precious for them. So I was their only chance to change this custom.

Would I agree to receive just one hindquarter, plus one share of the remainder? That way the shares for each man would be significantly larger and a new and fairer custom could be initiated. My command of the Magar language was still rather poor, and I didn't know how to properly question or negotiate in the Magar way. I was more than dubious about this changing-the-custom argument, and I was certain that they were taking advantage of me. But, on this happy day I didn't want to argue with them, so I consented.

A couple days later, however, the story behind the story slowly began to leak out. I had broken the hunters' curse. I had become the village's secret hero. Eleven years earlier a witch had cursed the hunters and since that day they had not killed a single animal. No one had been able to break the curse. But now I had. That was why the hunters had been so ecstatic.

Indeed, from that day onwards and for years to come they would once again successfully hunt Peak-of-the-gods. On good years they would harvest over twenty animals, but more regularly it was fifteen or so. Year after year they continued to kill fifteen to twenty animals, whereas for eleven years they had gotten nothing. *Zero.* Furthermore, in addition to breaking the curse, I had also changed their custom to one which brought about a more equal sharing of the treasured meat.

I had known nothing about these things at the time, but God did. For the next twenty years I hunted with them, and though Jipan shot a number of animals with my .22 rifle, I myself never shot another deer.

> *"The steps of a good man are ordered by the*
> *Lord, and He delights in his way."*
> Psalm 37:23

—Postscript—

Actually, it had taken quite a bit of gentle prying and persistent questioning on my part to ferret out the hunters' curse. The villagers did not talk openly about these things. They were fearful that another curse might be put upon them.

In the ensuing years, when Barbara and I faced multiple hardships and trials, I would be tempted to wonder whether God was doing anything or not. Then I would remember the footprints in the snow and the wrong-way deer that had come up the mountain towards the beaters. Despite the meager response to our efforts in Arakhala, we were determined to keep on and to be faithful to the call. We had to trust that God was at work in ways that we could not see. We had to remain content, even if most of the time we did not understand. If we persevered and did not give up, God would be free to build His Kingdom in His way.

Poap Bahadur and Michael with mountain goat

CHAPTER 10

THE EMPTY SEAT

Barbara had disappeared! Where had she gone? She was no longer on the back of my motorbike!

In Kathmandu the morning sun had not yet broken through the damp winter fog blanketing the valley. From our front yard there was a steep, grass-covered ramp that led up to a wide gate. Under the gate, a line of cement had been laid to keep stray dogs from getting in. The monsoon rains, however, had washed away much of the ramp's dirt leaving a large cement bump across the entrance under the gate.

At night, we always kept the gate closed. But there was no fixed rule for the daytime and sometimes it was left open, as it had been this morning. When we started out together on our little Honda Trail Bike, Barbara sat sidesaddle on the rack behind me and grasped hold of it. (In those days it was absolutely against social mores for women to touch men in public.)

In order to climb the driveway I had to give the little bike full power, but I also had to slow to a near stop when we crossed the threshold. Too little speed and I would stall. Too much speed and we would go flying. This time I did it perfectly, and we rolled smoothly over the hump.

I made a tight right turn and we started across town. The road was congested with people carrying their vegetables and goods to market. There were also cows and even an occasional bull wandering about or lying in the roadway. I proceeded slowly down the little dirt road, concentrating hard on keeping the bike balanced while I negotiated the large potholes.

It was noisy in the crowded narrow lane and I was speaking loudly to tell Barbara something or other as we went along. Three or four minutes later, we arrived at Asan Tole Bazaar where the jam of bodies forced me to stop. It was then that I noticed I didn't seem to have much difficulty balancing the bike. Looking back, Barbara was nowhere to be seen. I was really puzzled and assumed that she had slipped off just as we had entered the crowded bazaar. When I couldn't find her, I turned around and made my way back towards home, wondering where she could be.

When I got back, there she was standing by the gate! "What are you doing here?" I asked.

Well, she had bailed off to shut the gate. Since the gate was already open, I had assumed that we were keeping it open, but she had thought that it should be closed. Just as we topped the bump, she had slid off in such a way that I didn't feel the shift in weight.

It amazes me how a small difference in assumptions can lead to a parting of ways. I thought she was still with me and therefore continued on, not knowing that I was alone in my journey. I was so focused on avoiding dogs, kids, and potholes, or from hitting people, cows, push carts, and rickshaws, that I never noticed that the seat was empty. Furthermore, with a helmet on my head and the cacophony of sounds around me, I wasn't really expecting to hear a response to what I was saying. And certainly, I did not.

This reminded me how often I had promised, "Jesus, I will follow!" Though I may have begun the day with Jesus, I had gotten so caught up with avoiding the potholes in front of me, or solving the problems of the day, that I didn't think to ask Him for an opinion. Worse, I didn't even expect to hear from Him. Only occasionally would I realize that I had been driving on alone. Jesus had wanted me to stop somewhere. He had had something for me to do, and when I didn't, it was as if He had jumped off to wait for me to return.

> *"I called, but you did not answer,*
> *I spoke, but you did not listen."*
> Isaiah 65:12

CHAPTER 11

HEALING HANDS
❧❧❧

Suddenly I had the strangest feeling. What was happening? It seemed as if everything in my body was becoming sick all at once. Then slowly, across my back, an unusual pain began to develop. I took some aspirin... but the pain continued to escalate. Then I took some codeine. That didn't help, either.

It had all begun as just a normal spring morning in Arakhala. Adina was 19 months old and Barbara was two months pregnant with Michael. April can be very warm in Arakhala and I was wearing shorts, a t-shirt, and flip-flops. In the hot weather we really appreciated our home's thick walls of mud and rock, as well as its heavy grass roof, which helped to keep us relatively cool.

As the pain worsened I began to get desperate. Barbara searched through our Wycliffe Medical Manual, and it soon became clear that I was suffering from a kidney stone attack. Across the mountains there was a little mission clinic run by Gwen Coventry and

Elfriede Bernhardt. That was our only hope. Writing a short note, I asked them for some morphine or their strongest pain medicine.

Then I made my way down through the village to Jipan's house and asked him to send a runner over immediately. Magars who have grown up in a land of steep mountains and deep gorges develop tremendous stamina. A Magar man could average more than 1,500 feet an hour while climbing or descending the rugged terrain. If he wasn't delayed, I knew he could get there and back in about eight hours.

Slowly, I made my way back up the trail to our house. Bent double like an old man and perspiring profusely from the excruciating pain, I paused to vomit beside the trail. Back home Barbara and I discussed what to do. We had only one way to get additional help and that was to send a telegram to evacuate us. It would take two full days for a runner to reach Narayanghat, the nearest town, if he weren't held up. Our hope was that the telephone lines to Kathmandu would not be down and that the telegram would actually be delivered to our group office on the same day it arrived. They would then make arrangements for a plane. After buzzing our village, the pilot would wait for a few hours on our tiny airstrip in the valley while I was carried down. From the time the runner left, we could hope that a plane might rescue me within four or five days... if everything went just right.

It was already too late to find someone to go that day, so we decided to wait until the next morning. Meanwhile, all the codeine I dared to take was not helping. The pain was relentless. It was simply unbearable. Moaning and groaning, I rolled back and forth on the floor, uselessly trying to find a little relief somehow, someway. Then Barbara put her hands on me and began to pray. Almost immediately, I lost consciousness.

I awoke about half an hour later and the pain was gone. We presumed the kidney stone had passed into my bladder and indeed it had. But just to be sure that it was gone, whenever I urinated, I did so into a cup. Two days later, I was greatly relieved when I heard a *plink*. Sure enough, there was the little rascal... the size of a grain of rice, football-shaped, and covered with spines. I had never needed the medicine that arrived that night from Gwen and Elfriede.

> *"And these signs will accompany those who*
> *believe...*
> *they will place their hands on sick people,*
> *and they will get well."*
> Mark 16:17-18

—Postscript—

Six weeks after the kidney stone attack we returned to Kathmandu with Baju, the old derelict who had been assigned by the village leaders to be our Magar teacher. In February I had had infectious hepatitis, and on our return to Kathmandu, I was diagnosed with amoebic hepatitis. Then in July, I contracted mononucleosis and as soon as I had the strength to travel, we left Nepal... in my opinion, never to return again.

Leaving Nepal—Sept. 5, 1973

—Recovery in America—

(1973-1974)

CHAPTER 12

THE MOOSE

❧❧❧

"Blessed are those whose strength is in you..."
Psalm 84:5

He was coming at me with long strides and when I finally saw him, the Bull Moose was nearly upon me!

Two months earlier, God had preserved my life as I lay dying from liver failure in Kathmandu. When I got strong enough to travel, we left Nepal and went straight to my parents' home in Oak Harbor, Washington. After a five year absence, Dad was obviously distressed to see me so weak and debilitated. Nevertheless, a few days later he came to me rather excited. He wanted me to join him and his cronies on their big moose hunt up in Canada!

To me, his suggestion seemed almost absurd, but I didn't want to disappoint Dad. All year long he looked forward to their annual hunt, and usually he and his friends would fill their freezers with good meat for the winter.

By then I was without pain and looking okay, but there was unseen injury to my body. Somehow, the nerves in my neck and shoulders had become seriously damaged. They were so weak that to keep my coffee cup from spilling, I needed two hands to steady it. Nonetheless, I decided to go along with Dad, if I were able.

But how could I hunt? How could I hold up a heavy rifle with the muscles in my neck and shoulders atrophying? "Never mind," I thought, "it is God's problem to fulfill the plans He has for me."

Eight years earlier God had promised me "life more abundantly." Though my body had deteriorated terribly, I remained fully certain that His ability to do the impossible had not changed. As the time of the hunt grew closer, I noticed that I was beginning to gain a little strength. But to recover, I still had a long, long way to go.

A week before leaving, I took Dad's rifle out. I couldn't lift it up in the normal way, so I put the butt of the gun to my shoulder. Then I tried swinging the gun. I managed to get the barrel up level, but the rifle came right back down. The day before we left, I tried again. This time I swung the gun hard, and for a split second I was able to keep it somewhat level. That was an improvement, but of course I could never aim and shoot accurately, like that.

After a two-day drive north into the wilderness of British Columbia, we reached the end of the road where we stayed in Bob's little log cabin. By law we were required to hunt with a guide, and Bob had lived there all his life. He would usually take two hunters out on horses for one day, then another two hunters out the following day. Dad had shot many a moose, so he wanted me to hunt in his place with Pete Suda, while he did the cooking. On Sunday, the first day of our hunt, I offered to take my turn the following day. Dad's friends, Ralph West and Joe Johnson, were okay with that. So it was on Monday morning that Dad held up two straws in his hand, and I gave Pete the honor of picking which of us would shoot first. Pete selected the short straw. I would shoot in the morning and he would shoot in the afternoon.

Stamina and strength were my challenge. I could sit on a horse by then, but I couldn't hold the rifle to my shoulder for more than a moment. How would I manage it? Or rather, I wondered, how would God manage it?

The previous day, Bob had led Ralph and Joe through many miles of deep spruce forest and they had not seen a single moose. So this morning, Bob decided to hunt a nearby mountain. Unfortunately, however, the hoar frost was so heavy that the thick ice crunching beneath the horses' feet could be heard from a great distance. This seemed to make our chances pretty hopeless.

About 10:30 a.m., we neared the top of the mountain and Bob decided that the only way we would get close to a moose was to leave our horses and hunt on foot. Soon we came across fresh tracks. Indeed, moose were in the area. Slipping quietly through the forest, I followed Bob, and Pete followed me. As we skirted the top of a ravine, a cow moose appeared. She passed us by as we stood motionless in the forest.

A minute later, we were picking our way through some alder brush when an animal began to appear out of the steep ravine to my left. I couldn't see it clearly and backing up a few steps, I saw a bull moose closing in on me quickly. As I had practiced, I swung the rifle up. Momentarily, the gun steadied. The crosshairs of the scope were centered just above the bull's heart. I squeezed the trigger and the bull reversed ends and disappeared. Slowly, cautiously, we moved forward and there he was… stone dead at the bottom of the ravine.

Bob was elated. His previous client had hunted for eight days and had gone home empty-handed. Stepping off the distance, the moose had been only 25 yards away. Bob exclaimed that I should never expect to get this close to a bull moose again, even if I hunted with him for another thirty years. Later in the day, Pete shot a larger bull—also his first moose. That was the end of my hunt. It had entailed a two day drive, a three-hour horseback ride, a pleasant, thirty-minute stroll in the beautiful virgin forest, and a lifting of Dad's rifle for a split second.

—Postscript—

This was the first, and ultimately, the only moose I have ever bagged. Ralph and Joe hunted for another six days and never shot a thing. When I had left for Nepal in 1969, I had turned my back on an exciting life filled with hunting and fishing, and I was okay

with that. It was just part of the sacrifice I had determined to make in order to bring the message of peace
and joy to an unknown people. Now, having cheated
death by the narrowest of margins, I had returned
home a failure and in complete weakness. God,
however, used this hunting trip as an opportunity
to show me His love in a uniquely meaningful way.
Furthermore, He gave me the privilege of partici-
pating in His promise that states: *"My strength is
made perfect in weakness,"* (2 Corinthians 12:9).

CHAPTER 13

IN THE GAP

*"I looked for a man among them who would
build up the wall and stand before me in the
gap on behalf of the land..."*
Ezekiel 22:30

In the fall of 1967, Barbara and I had enrolled at Canadian Bible College in Regina, Saskatchewan. We planned to take a few Bible courses before we headed to Mexico for six months at Wycliffe's Jungle Camp. God, however, had a larger plan. That plan was to find someone who would hear His call to stand in the gap.

Ervin and Adina Bergmann were also there at this time and we became fast friends. Ervin went on to pastor a small church in northern Canada, and we went overseas. While in Nepal, we wrote to one another regularly and we named our first child after Adina.

We had expected to be gone for five years. That was standard in those days. But sicknesses cut our time short. In February of 1973, both Barbara and I came down with hepatitis. After getting some strength back we returned to Arakhala in April. We weren't there long before I had a kidney stone attack. In May, I contracted amoebic dysentery. By the time we got back to Kathmandu, the amoebas had migrated to my liver resulting in amoebic hepatitis. Fortunately, the parasites had not migrated to my brain. The medicine made quick work of them, but we didn't realize how much my liver had been damaged.

In late July, I contracted a severe throat infection. Some days later I began to experience a relentless pain between my shoulders, and then in my triceps. When I could endure it no longer, I was rushed to Shanta Bhawan Hospital. Ten days passed before tests confirmed that I had mononucleosis. Meanwhile, Dr. Strong must have understood that my liver was failing, because he gave me handfuls of pills. Ten years later I met Dr. Strong's wife, Patricia, and learned that he had come home night after night telling her that I might be gone by morning!

Back in Canada, Ervin had received my letter asking him to pray for Baju, a depraved old soldier, who had just become our language helper. One day Ervin was walking through his church's sanctuary when he heard God speak in his spirit, "Gary is in mortal danger!"

Immediately, he went to the altar where he prayed for two hours. Day after day and week after week

Ervin kept praying, building up a wall of protection for me as he interceded for my life.

In those days, phone contact was expensive and involved shouting loudly. Even then, one was usually not understood. Letters might make it in 25-35 days. As usual, when one is in crisis he doesn't have time or energy to write others. Other than God's certain voice, no one had communicated with Ervin about my condition.

Arriving home in the U.S., I was still very weak. Some months later when we were visiting them, Ervin told me about his experience. Putting it all together, we realized that Ervin had prayed through my crisis and hadn't stopped until I had turned the corner and left the hospital. No one else in America told us of hearing with their spiritual ears about my danger. But at a small church in Northern Canada, God had found someone who would stand in the gap.

—Postscript—

I am acutely aware of our desperate need to have faithful partners who "look after the baggage" when we go out to do battle with the Kingdom of Darkness. King David made it clear at Ziklag that: *"The share of the man who stayed with the supplies is to be the same as that of him who went down to the battle. All will share alike,"* (1 Samuel 30:24).

In the spirit realm, I believe that principle applies as well, for those who pray for others.

CHAPTER 14

THE GREAT BURDEN

I had not realized it, but over the years it had grown into a heavy, debilitating burden...

It was November 6, 1973, and we had been with Wycliffe for 6½ years, 4½ of them in Nepal. Our plan was to learn an unknown language in a remote part of the world, to help the people in practical ways, and to share with them our hope—the joy of walking with Jesus.

We began working with the Magar people in the mountains of Central Nepal, but it was more difficult than we had expected. I was not particularly quick at learning a foreign language. Barbara's A+ abilities, however, had convinced the Wycliffe leaders to send us, presuming that Barbara would carry the majority of the language work. That was okay. I decided I would persevere and do my best.

A Magar village was located, and we moved to Yangchok in November of 1969. The people were friendly and helpful. However, the Brahmin influence was strong, and we, as *untouchables*, were not even allowed to enter the house of the lowly Magars. The most serious roadblock occurred, however, in finding a faithful language helper. The people were always busy working in their fields just to have something to eat, and though I happily paid anyone who would help us, we were never able to find someone to teach us consistently. In order to learn Magar, we followed the villagers out to the forests and fields and did whatever they were doing. That was sufficient to start with, but soon we needed to begin analyzing the Magar grammar and putting this unwritten language on paper. For that, we needed an assistant who would go over long lists of phrases and sentences with us... and for a long time, that didn't happen.

After 2½ years, we moved from Yangchok Village to Arakhala where there were no Brahmins. There, at least, we had better exposure to the language, but still no language helper. In September 1971, Adina was born and Barbara could no longer maintain the same pace with the language work. I was doing all the village medical work, leaving her free to concentrate on the language. Now, however, we decided to switch roles, and she looked after the villagers' medical needs.

Wycliffe's five-year goal for us translators was to analyze the basic grammar and translate the Gospel of Mark before we returned home for furlough. We had some brainy friends working with other tribal languages, and there was always that niggling feeling that maybe I wasn't doing enough. Collegues in other tribes had language helpers and were moving ahead, but we felt that we were proceeding at a crawl.

Then there were the innumerable incidents of sickness. I don't remember how many different diseases worked us over, or how many times we had parasites or dysentery, but they were regular events. Each time it wore us down and slowed our progress a little bit more.

In February 1973, both Barbara and I came down with infectious hepatitis and in April there was my kidney stone attack. Then in May, the village leaders assigned us a language helper, but to my great dismay, old Thapa Baju appeared to be a complete derelict!

When we returned to Kathmandu in June, I contracted amoebic hepatitis. The one thing, however, that encouraged us in those days was Thapa Baju. Contrary to my initial expectations, Baju turned out to be an excellent helper and most interested in reading the Nepali New Testament. Before we got very far, however, I came down with a strep throat and then mononucleosis.

We sent Baju back to Arakhala and made plans to return to the U.S. We were going home without translating a single chapter of scripture. Before we left, our director asked me to return within six months to keep our work moving forward. I mumbled weakly that I would, but I lied. I had no intention of returning at all.

On September 7, 1973, my parents met us at the little airfield near our home in Oak Harbor, Washington. After five years they were very happy to see us again, but very concerned about me.

Barbara was due to give birth to Michael in December, so we went to stay with her folks in San Diego, California. In early November we learned that Chaplin Merlin Carothers was speaking in nearby Lemon Grove. We had been encouraged by his recent book, <u>Prison</u> <u>to</u> <u>Praise</u>. Immediately after speaking, however, he went home, leaving his assistants to pray for those with needs.

When my turn came, I was ministered to by Ezra, a large fellow from New Zealand. I became rather disappointed, however, when he seemed to ignore all my physical problems. Instead, he asked me to take my burdens and sorrows, wrap them up in a bundle, and lay them at the foot of the Cross. As he prayed, I did that in my mind, and immediately I felt a *huge* load lift from my shoulders. When he finished praying, he told me that as my spirit slowly recovered, so would my physical body. And it happened just as he said. I never recovered from all the muscle damage to my neck, shoulders, and arms, but it was enough.

In retrospect, I had been focusing on my physical problems, but in ministering to me, Ezra discerned my emotional and spiritual exhaustion. He had the wisdom to know that if I would only lay that great burden of failure and care at the Cross, Jesus would do all the rest.

> *"Cast all your cares upon Him,*
> *for He cares for you!"*
> 1 Peter 5:7

CHAPTER 15

THE TWELVE

"He is always wrestling in prayer for you that you may stand firm in all the will of God.."
Colossians 4:12

Nope, I wouldn't be returning to Nepal. Why, I thought, would I go back there just to die?

That was my assessment in the months before the TWELVE came into our lives. I had come home physically and emotionally exhausted. The series of sicknesses I had encountered during our last six months in Nepal had been the last straw. The result had been that major nerves along my spine were damaged, and now the skin on my back was without sensation and the muscles of my neck, triceps, and shoulders were atrophying.

It was an unrelenting stress to live in a country that persecuted Christians. Just about everything we wanted to accomplish appeared to be suspect to the authorities. We had gone to a remote village in the mountains of Central Nepal and had expected to be *overcomers* (1 John 2:14). However, since the beginning of time (as far as we could tell) only Darkness had ruled there. In fact, it was we who had been overcome... escaping, so it seemed, only with our lives.

Convalescing back home in the U.S., I had lots of time to think. "Who," I wondered, "had benefited from our efforts?"

Sure, we had relieved incredible suffering for many in the villages and had saved innumerable lives with our medicine. We had also helped them build the first drinking water system, as well as significantly improving their crop production. Yes, we had hoped and prayed for many, but it had seemed that overall we had made very little difference.

We had learned that the Magar culture had many traits that were most admirable. Among them was a marriage system which protected women, and a family and village cohesiveness which helped everyone. Nevertheless, they appeared greatly oppressed by a system of witches and witchdoctors that kept them living in constant fear. The endless demand for an enormous number of animal sacrifices did much to reduce them to poverty. All but one, it seemed, remained shackled by these fears. Only old Thapa Baju might have done the radical thing and decided to follow Jesus. But even of that, we were not certain.

As my strength slowly returned, I began to analyze why we had had so many difficulties in Nepal. Our financial support had been adequate, and occasionally we even had some extra to share when colleagues had pressing needs. What I now discovered, however, was that those who sent us money were not necessarily prayer intercessors as well. And considering the powerful spiritual opposition we faced, somehow it felt like we had been thrown out to the wolves.

In my condition, it was obvious that I wasn't going anywhere soon. Consequently, there was no urgency to tell anyone that we did not plan to return. Then, in November of 1973, I experienced a breakthrough at a Merlin Carothers' meeting when I laid all these sorrows and burdens at the foot of the Cross.

I was not worried about our future. My dad would be overjoyed if I wanted to work with him and we returned to Oak Harbor. I knew I could make plenty of money. But what was God's plan? In the following weeks, as I talked to the Lord about our future, the thought came to me that we could return to Nepal and actually survive. However, to do so, it was essential that we have more friends who would seriously pray for us.

One day I made a secret contract with the Lord. I decided that, other than discussing it with Barbara, I would say nothing to others about quitting Wycliffe, nor would I mention the deal I had made with God. I was willing to return if He would bring at least twelve people who would pray for us diligently. Just a little while later, dear Bill Christy, a retired missionary, told me that he had been impressed by God to especially pray for us when we went back to Nepal. That was ONE. A couple weeks later, another person told me the same. That was TWO for my list.

As the months went by, one person here and another person there continued to be added to my list, including Thelma Raymond, who was a secretary. I arranged to write her regularly from Nepal, and she promised to type up carbon copies and to mail them to the others. When Barbara and I boarded the plane in October 1974, my secret list had exactly twelve names.

As time went on, others were added to the list. However, I don't think I'll ever forget the original "twelve" who were unaware of my contract with God. The unsolicited twelve who volunteered to stand in the gap for us. Twelve willing individuals without whom our life among the Magars would have ended. Just twelve individuals... without whom the Magar people would not have a New Testament.

> *"Be alert and always keep on praying*
> *for all the saints."*
> Ephesians 6:18

—Return to Nepal—

(1974-1986)

CHAPTER 16

THE BEGGAR MAN

It happened in Kathmandu in the spring of 1975. We were living in Kalimati in a house that faced the main road. Late one morning I heard someone rattling our iron gate, which in that culture was the equivalent of ringing our doorbell. Beggars, vegetable sellers, and others rattled it throughout the day to get our attention. If they were beggars, we usually gave them a cup of rice. That was the appropriate, if not generous, thing to do.

Surprisingly, this beggar immediately set his price. He wanted three rupees to buy a whole meal. Dressed in simple village clothing, I readily recognized him as a man from the Tamang tribe. Somehow his demeanor seemed different than the regular beggars, so I asked what his problem was. He claimed to have come in by bus to sell a load of bananas. But last night while he was sound asleep, someone had stolen his money, his hat, and his flip-flops.

Once he got something to eat, he said he would start walking back home. By taking a shortcut through the high passes, he could reach his village in 48 hours. I questioned him about the cost of a bus ticket to Trisuli from whence he had come. If he really had come in by bus, he would know the price. He did. After a few more questions, I ascertained that his story was probably true.

So instead of three rupees, I handed him the price of a bus ticket. He looked puzzled and simply replied that the next bus wouldn't be leaving until tomorrow morning. I told him I knew that, so... here were three rupees for a meal now... plus money for lunch... plus money for dinner tonight... and money for food tomorrow. He seemed grateful and left.

But two weeks later he was back, rattling our gate again! When I saw him there, I felt rather annoyed that he would come back and beg for more. This time he was wearing a new hat, had new flip-flops and was carrying a young rooster in his arms. Hiding my irritation, I asked him about his trip home and learned that all had gone well. Though just a simple villager, he was an enterprising fellow and had returned with yet another load of bananas to sell. "Here," he said, offering me the rooster, "this is repayment for what you gave me."

I replied that it was impossible for me to take his rooster. What I had given to him was given in God's name. How could I take a reward for what God had done? That made sense to him and he left, happily taking his chicken with him.

"Give to everyone who asks you...
Do to others as you would have them do to you."
Luke 6:30-31

Gary on the trail with Michael

CHAPTER 17

MUTTON FOR DINNER
❧❧❧

S omething was drastically wrong with our translation. Baju had no question in his mind—the
man had invited his neighbors over to eat the sheep.
But that, of course, was not the point of Jesus' story.
The Good Shepherd had left his ninety-nine sheep to
save the lost one. Not to go get it for dinner!

Baju, however, couldn't be budged. Jesus said
that the shepherd had returned home with the animal
rejoicing, and he had invited his neighbors over to
eat it. Wasn't a central part of Jesus' teaching about
giving and sharing? When they themselves found
their lost animal that's what they would do—they
would share it.

I was really puzzled. There was nothing difficult about the story and we had translated it clearly.
Coaching him that the point was not to eat the sheep,
I read the story to Baju a second and a third time. He,
however, continued to insist that they were going to
eat the sheep.

We had translated the Gospel of Luke, and Kent Gordon, our best translation consultant, had checked it all very meticulously. It was up to me, however, to do in-depth comprehension checks and to catch any glitches that had slipped by. In a tribal culture, miscommunication can creep in at the most unexpected places. On the surface the words may be plain, but the meaning and interpretation of them can be so very different.

They would share... that's what they would do. After all, they had no electricity, no refrigeration. If you had some meat, you would share it with your neighbors. It was a regular event on those rugged mountainsides. Often, you couldn't see between the brush and trees further than 50 feet. So it wasn't difficult for jackals or a leopard to slip in and kill one or more of your animals.

Those animals are most valuable. They are your very bank account. Meat, too, is scarce and expensive in these poor villages. If you discovered an animal missing, you would immediately begin to search in earnest. If it hadn't been gone for long, you might find the lost animal and bring it back alive. But just as often, you would only find the spot where it had been killed.

Jackals move off their kill straight away, but leopards protest. With a lot of shouting and beating of sticks, however, the growling leopard would back away and you could recover your animal. Women or children wouldn't dare to confront a large leopard, but the Magar men certainly would. Since leopards often like to play around with their kill before settling in for dinner, if it hadn't been too long, you could often recover the whole carcass. But whole or a piece, you would return home quite happy. Tonight there would be meat for dinner!

Feeling a bit frustrated, I told Baju: "Look, I'm reading it again and we are **not** going to eat the sheep!"

"Whatever." That was fine with him.

So, slowly and deliberately, I began reading through the text again. Then Baju interrupted me, "The sheep is dead. Of course they'll eat the sheep!"

"What! We've said nothing in the story about dying. How can the sheep be dead?"

"Well, he carried the sheep on his shoulder," Baju answered. "You can't carry a live animal on your shoulder. How can you do that? If he carried it on his *shoulder*, the animal is dead!"

"How do you carry a live animal then?" I asked.

"Around your *neck*, of course… so you can grasp all four legs."

So, we changed out one single word. We replaced shoulder with the word for neck. Finished! The animal is now alive and the focus of Jesus' story shifts dramatically. The teaching is not about sharing, it is about the Shepherd, who risked his flock, risked his whole life's savings, in his determination to save that *one* which is lost.

Buddies—Poap Bahadur and Michael

CHAPTER 18

POINTY EARS

*"And having disarmed the (demon) powers
and authorities,
He made a public spectacle of them, triumphing
over them by the cross."*
Colossians 2:15

As usual, our house was full of villagers — sick people wanting medicine, as well as others who had just come to visit. So when Michael and little Poap Bahadur came flying in the door breathlessly, I didn't pay any attention. It was only later that I learned of their close encounter.

Arakhala Village is built on a steep outcropping that in earlier times would have been easy to defend from three directions. Our house sits at the top edge of the Village beside the main trail. On that warm spring day, five-year-old Michael and his inseparable little sidekick had wandered up that trail. They were throwing stones, climbing trees, and just investigating anything that looked interesting as they made their way to the great *chautara* about 300 yards from our house. This was a bench-like area made with large flat stones. It had been built long ago as a place for tired folks to rest their heavy loads. Here, at a little dip in the ridge, are two huge shade trees. For a radius of fifty feet or so the area is open and flat. Then the trail zigzags up the steeply rising ridge which leads to the pass two hours away. The immediate area is free of brush, large boulders and other obstructions.

When they arrived at the *chautara*, no one was around. All the villagers had gone out to work in their fields, and it was still too early for the people who carried loads of rice and other goods up from the plains to be passing through. In the course of just messing around as little boys do, they looked up to see that someone was there. Going away from them up the trail was a man seven feet tall. Villagers averaged 5' 4", so this man was a real giant. Furthermore, all his clothes were pitch black, including the superman-style cape that hung from his shoulders. Since villagers don't wear capes, this made him appear even more unusual.

Then the man stopped, turned around and stared at them. His long pointy ears were like Mr. Spock's in *Star Trek* and his eyes — they were bright red! In a flash the boys bolted for home. But then they stopped momentarily to look back. They needed to see where the giant was, but instead he had disappeared. Now they were really scared! Perhaps he was circling to get between them and the Village. They could be in deep trouble.

From the youngest age, Magar children carry heavy loads on their backs. In those mountains there is hardly a place flat enough to get out and really run, so their leg muscles develop for steep climbing over rugged ground, not for running. Consequently, at age five Michael could already outrun all but the largest kids.

But today was different. Today, Poap Bahadur's legs pumped faster and reached out further than at any other time in his life. Even a dim-wit knows that it is the last person in line who gets caught. As they sprinted down the broad trail for home, Michael poured on the speed to overtake his buddy. But when he pulled abreast of Poap, his friend's bare feet churned the dirt even faster. Fear pumped adrenalin into Michael's veins, and reaching inside himself for more speed, he began to pass his little pal again. But Poap had no intention of being the last man today, and he wasn't! The faster Michael went, the faster his friend's stubby little legs moved. Even today Michael is amazed over how he got that speed.

In those times, the people regularly, if not daily, saw demon appearances around the village. Usually they sighted them at dusk or in the early dawn. The daily gossip was usually over the circumstances that were involved with those appearances. The fear those manifestations engendered was very, very great. In fact, at night many grown men wouldn't dare to venture outside of their homes to relieve themselves without taking along a companion.

Ten or twelve years after this event, Poap became the first young man in Arakhala to join Baju in following Jesus. Baju was his close relative and lived only three houses away. For seventeen years he had watched and listened as Baju had continued to pursue God's way. Poap was determined not to be intimidated by fear of the witchdoctor, and nothing forced him to recant his decision. Consequently, little by little, others were also emboldened to join them in following Jesus.

It was when the number of believers began multiplying that those fearful demon appearances ended. It wasn't that the demons had all abandoned Arakhala. Rather, the believers supposed that they just became ashamed to show themselves. The Light of the World had come and the demons could not withstand it.

CHAPTER 19

THE DEADLY MEDICINE

Adina and Michael watched unconcerned as I loaded the syringe. Carefully, I nudged the plunger forward until all of the air bubbles were out of the needle... then I stabbed it into Michael's little buttock.

Growing up in Arakhala Village, Adina and Michael would often go barefoot like their friends. In fact, Adina would let her friends wear her flip-flops so that she had an excuse to go barefoot like them. As a result, our kids were always getting thorns, splinters, or cuts in their feet. And like their little friends, they quickly forgot their sores and wounds and went on with enjoying life.

However, since the village was filled with pig dung and every other kind of excreta, their feet often got infected. There was really nothing to be done about it, except to regularly remind them to have us apply an antiseptic to their injuries. But since hurting one's foot was such a common occurrence, our instructions were often forgotten. Occasionally we would warn them that if they let an infection go too long, it could turn into blood poisoning. Then they would be in big trouble. Michael and Adina would politely listen, but weren't overly impressed by Barbara's or my dire predictions. After all, none of their friends seemed bothered about it.

Lee Maya and Adina

One night I happened to see that Michael's foot had become infected—this time a bit deeper than usual. Once again I took the opportunity to warn them about blood poisoning. When we awoke the next morning, to my alarm, a bright red infected vein had already run up his leg to the top of his knee. A bit irritated I announced, "Alright, now you get a shot! In another twelve hours that infection will reach your heart, and then you will be dead!"

In Nepal, it seemed like we were always getting shots for one thing or another. As a very little fellow, Michael would naturally cry when he got a shot. But one day I told him about strong boys not crying and he bought the idea entirely. When it was his turn for the shot, he marched up like a little soldier and hardly flinched. From then onwards, whenever it came time for shots, he would try to be the first one in line to show how brave he was. And because he was relaxed and not fearful, the shot hurt him less.

In those days, we had a problem with penicillin powder. When it was mixed with the sterile water, it was thicker than the other medicines. Consequently, we had to use a large diameter needle, and even so, every so often the penicillin would get blocked in the needle. Disposable syringes weren't used in those days, so we had to twist the needle off the glass syringe and put another one on.

This time, as usual, Michael wasn't at all disturbed. But when I gave him the shot, the penicillin jammed in the needle. So, I pulled it out of his bottom and replaced the needle. With a new needle on the syringe, I expelled the air again and shot him in the other buttock. Michael never flinched, but again the medicine plugged the needle. This was really frustrating and becoming a bit scary. He desperately needed that penicillin to stop the blood infection. Pulling the needle out, I repeated the sequence and shot him in his skinny little arm. For a third time the needle jammed! This was too much for our brave little soldier, and he began to cry.

Three tries was enough for me, too, but now we were in a great dilemma. Barbara consulted our Wycliffe Medical Manual and found that we had an alternative medicine that might work in his case. She gave him the tablets and we watched him closely. Happily, the medicine acted quickly and the infection in his vein subsided the next day.

Never before or after did we experience the needle jamming three times, and perhaps we would have forgotten how strange that was. But a few months later, while we were in Kathmandu, Michael took ill and the doctor prescribed a course of oral penicillin. The next morning, Michael's skin was hot and red. Barbara immediately suspected an allergic reaction, and took him back to the doctor who confirmed it. Michael had become penicillin allergic!

Isolated out in Arakhala Village, I don't like to dwell on what could have happened if I had injected that large dose of penicillin into his little body. Clearly, once again, God had intervened on our behalf.

"The Angel of the Lord encamps around
those who fear Him, and He delivers them."
Psalm 34:7

—Postscript—

The victim of a penicillin reaction, like persons who are allergic to bee stings, can go into anaphylactic shock. This is a life-threatening event. The reaction may progress so rapidly that it leads to a collapse of the respiratory or cardiovascular system. With the long-acting type of penicillin we were using and our isolation, Michael's prognosis could have been extremely poor indeed.

Michael with chicken-eating snake

CHAPTER 20

THE BIG SNAKE

Michael was about five years old, and as usual, he was running down the trail in front of us. But ahead, in the streambed, camouflaged and motionless among the rocks, lay a huge snake.

It was the spring of 1978. Having been forced to leave Nepal in 1976, we had returned six months later and God had provided a visa for us through Barbara teaching at the Norwegian School. Now, a year later, we were back in Arakhala for a few weeks.

At this time, Baju was living in his little grass-roofed hut up on Peak-of-the-gods, and he had invited us over for a meal. To reach his home, however, we had to cross an enormous gorge. Up at daybreak we had eaten a little something and started down the trail. It would get hot before long, and we wanted to reach Baju's place while the trail was still in the shadow of the mountain. It was a steep 1,500 foot descent down to the stream and then a rugged 2,500 foot climb up to Baju's place.

Barbara and I were carrying our local *jholas*. In this shoulder bag we put water bottles, a couple of bananas, and some basic medicines to treat needy villagers whom we would inevitably meet during the day. As for hiking attire, all of us wore the same thing—cheap rubber flip flops. I would often take a strong stick for support on the difficult parts of a trip, but I had not taken one this day. I knew this trail well, and for us, the trip was less than three hours each way.

On our treks, Michael would always be so full of energy that for the first couple of hours at least, he would be running on ahead. Inevitably, he would jump out from behind a tree or a boulder and try to startle us. Or else, he would just be exploring and enjoying getting to the next switchback sooner than the rest. Then towards the end of the day, as his little legs began to move at a slower pace, he would end up dragging along behind. Adina was just the opposite. She would typically start out slow, but later in the day, having conserved her energy and eager to reach our destination, she would surge on ahead of us.

At this time of the year, the water in the stream at the bottom of the gorge had largely dried up. There the rough trail meandered through the brush and around large rocks that had been deposited by the monsoon floods. It was here, some fifteen feet ahead of me, that I saw the snake on the trail—nearly as big around as my wrist! He was dark grayish in color and blended in perfectly with the rocks. Michael had already passed the snake and I was afraid that he might come racing back through the bushes and run into it. As I jolted to a stop, I must have made some sort of disturbance for the snake began to slither very slowly off the trail.

I looked around for a stick, but there was nothing. I looked for a rock, but they were either too large or just pebbles. The idea was useless, however, for by the time I finally did find a stone, I was shaking so badly that I couldn't throw it properly.

It all turned out to be a non-event. Michael had never seen it. Running along as he did and jumping from rock to rock, he had gone right over the top of the snake. Had he been injected with poison by such a large snake, there would have been no hope for him at all. We would have lost our only son.

But God knew what we didn't know and saw what we didn't see. He had protected us and kept us from all harm... for which we are forever grateful.

"And surely I will be with you always, even to the very end of the age."
Matthew 28:20

CHAPTER 21

THE TRAIN CONDUCTOR
❧❧❧

O ur passports, our money, and our plane tickets were gone! What was I going to do now?

It was October 1979, and we were in Huahin, Thailand, enjoying the beach. It was such a great place to be with Barbara's parents for a much-needed break from the tensions and heavy stresses in Nepal. Now, however, our time was coming to an end. But before her parents went back to San Diego and we returned to Nepal, Barbara and her mother wanted to shop for bargains in Bangkok. So, they took the bus leaving Ham and me to come up later with the kids. It was a real win-win situation.

We, however, decided to forego the bus. Instead, we thought to give Adina and Michael a treat and go up to Bangkok by train. We didn't know, however, that this day was a big holiday, and oodles of school kids and families would be traveling. Fortunately, we had reserved seats and though people were packed shoulder to shoulder on the train, it didn't matter much to us. We opened the compartment window and the kids ever so much enjoyed their first train ride.

Barbara and Lucille had traveled light and had left us in charge of all the bags. That was okay—we made a plan for unloading them during the short three-minute stop in Bangkok. Ham and the kids got off and came around to the open window. Then, I passed the suitcases out to them. The plan worked smoothly, despite the crowds of people. After carefully surveying the empty compartment, I hurried off the train. The first thing we did was to move our luggage to the middle of the platform and pile it up against a column. Once the great surge of people had subsided, we would figure out how to get it to a taxi. Meanwhile, Adina had taken upon herself Mommy's job of supervising the luggage. And just as Mommy did, Adina now counted the bags. When she finished, she announced that we were one bag short!

I knew she must be wrong, so we counted again, and yet again. I couldn't believe it! We were still one short. But it wasn't just a suitcase, it was the one which contained our passports, our traveler's checks, plane tickets, and extra money. I had to get back on the train and find it! By now, however, the train had started moving... and I wasn't able to push through the crowd fast enough.

Stunned, I stood among the great press of humanity, watching the train pull away from the station. What would I do now? For some reason, it never occurred to me that the bag might have been stolen. But then, a couple of minutes later, a train conductor emerged from the mass of people and set down our missing suitcase. Ham had Thai money in his pocket and I asked him to give the conductor a generous tip. But the man shook his head, "No!" He wouldn't take a tip and turning away, he disappeared back into the crowd. My mind was completely over- whelmed. I was reeling in shock, disbelief, astonish- ment, anguish, relief, and rejoicing all at the same moment!

Later, as we talked about the incident, it seemed even stranger. How did that conductor know this was our bag? If he had, why didn't he open it and take the valuables? Where did he get it? I was 100% certain that it was not left in our compartment. And how could he find us in such a crowd? Finally, why would a poorly paid government employee refuse a tip which could have doubled his day's wage?

All in all, we began to sense the fragrance of heaven's servants.

> *"Are not all angels ministering spirits*
> *sent to serve those who will inherit*
> *salvation?"*
> Hebrews 1:14

CHAPTER 22

THE BEARS

*"Ask and you shall receive
that your joy may be full."*
John 16:24

" *B*ha-lu-ke jhu-gu-dik-cho," Baju repeated excitedly.

Since he had left Arakhala Village three days earlier, he had been bursting to tell me the amazing thing that God had done. Before he could come to work with us in Kathmandu that summer, Baju had first needed to get his corn harvested. His only son was in India with the Gurkha Forces, and it was up to him to see that all went well at home. Now in August of 1981, the corn was in and he had finally arrived.

It wasn't too unusual for Baju to get excited like this. As soon as I had opened the door, he was exclaiming the story's conclusion without even telling me the story. This was not the first time it had happened, so I knew that it was better not to ask him anything at the moment. Bringing Baju inside, I got him to sit down and had Meena, our house helper, make us a cup of tea. Since he had already told me the conclusion, Baju's excitement had settled a bit. Never mind that I had no idea what he was talking about! So now I inquired, "How is it that the bears have been outwitted?"

I knew from our many years with the Magars that these poor villagers seldom, if ever, harvested enough corn to feed their families for the whole year. Often there was drought and sometimes even too much rain. On top of that, predators of every type took their toll. First there were crows, magpies, and parrots. Then there were the porcupines, civet cats, jackals, and monkeys. Finally, there were both the Himalayan and Sloth bears, which in a single night could destroy large sections of a field.

Between Arakhala Village and Peak-of-the-gods lies a rugged gorge. Across the gorge, Baju and his wife lived in a small thatched hut next to their fields. Baju's land was right up against the forest, so they were particularly vulnerable to predators. The chief problem was that their corn had to be completely dried on the stalk before it could be picked for storage. So from the time the corn kernels ripen, there is a three-week interval for it to mature and dry out. During this period, it seems like every wild creature on the mountain eats as much of it as they can!

Baju's faith had been growing and one of his favorite verses had become, *"Ask and you shall receive."* So it was that after his land had been plowed that spring, Baju decided to ask God for something he had never thought of before. The morning they were to begin planting, he told his wife, Kissery, to bring him the corn seed. Sitting on the ground, he put his arms around the woven grass basket and prayed, "Lord, this land, these fields, all belong to You. Bring the sun and bring the rain. Keep the predators from our fields."

Family with village girls—Dec. 1979

And just like Baju had asked, the rain had come at good intervals, as had the sun. When the corn began ripening, someone spent the day guarding their fields from the birds and monkeys. But during the night the fields were vulnerable. In previous years, the bears had made a regular habit of fattening themselves on Baju's corn. This year was different. Each morning when they surveyed their land, it was apparent that the bears had not yet arrived.

One day, Baju checked their corn and found that it had dried sufficiently. So old Baju, his wife, and the two orphans they were raising went out with their huge baskets. By nightfall, it had all been brought back to their hut. Then, that very night, the bears arrived. Finding no corn in Baju's fields, the bears continued down the mountain and ate their fill from the fields of Shami, the witch.

Baju had experienced great mercy and love from his Heavenly Father, and whenever I asked him what he thought had occurred in the spiritual realm, he was seldom without a ready answer. I am sure he thought me a bit dense in such matters, but he never once pointed it out. So when I asked him how it was that he had *fooled the bears*, he replied, "Well, of course! God sent his angels to guard the fields. After all, that is what I asked for."

He explained that every night when the bears had come down from the forest to eat, the angels would simply shoo them away. But after his corn had been harvested, of course, the angels had left for another assignment. Thus it was that when there were no guards to keep the bears away, they had rambled right down into his fields, just as they had always done. But when they found no corn on the stalks, they had continued on down the mountain until they got to Shami's fields and had eaten her corn instead.

A few years later, I talked with Baju about the bears. More and more of the forest was being destroyed and wildlife populations were declining;

nevertheless, bears still remained a problem. Baju told me that the bears had not eaten one bit of his corn since that day when he had asked God to post a guard. To my knowledge, the bears never again feasted on Baju's fields.

—Postscript—

Baju greatly loved the Book of Revelation because it tells the end of the story. The outcome of our battle against Satan is clear: We win!! It never bothered Baju in the least that the conclusion was revealed... before the whole story has been told.

CHAPTER 23

THE GOVERNOR

"*Ken-tek, ken-tek, ken-tek.*" Baju's crutches struck the hard rocky dirt as he toiled up the steep mountain trail. Ahead, pistol in belt, the police sergeant was leading the way to the police station at Dhobadi.

Of course, Baju was 100% guilty and he knew it. That didn't bother him as much as you might have thought. He was not one to let difficult circumstances dictate the presence of God. He was, however, greatly concerned for me.

Three months earlier they had come for Prem and his two friends who lived on the next ridge over. One had lost an eye in the beating and was never to recover his strength. He was to die a premature death just a few years later. Prem, himself, had been unable to walk for a whole month and was left with a lifetime of pain.

Would they beat him at that police station, Baju wondered? Would they be as merciless as they had been to his friends? Would they extract from him the information that by reading a Bible he had become a follower of Jesus? Would they learn that he had acquired that book at my house? That information, he knew, could put me out of Nepal and bring an end to our work.

The village witchdoctor, of course, had brought a charge against him. A little money slipped into the hands of the police was the usual for this sort of thing. The police were more than happy to help out. And so, late that morning a policeman had showed up at Baju's dirt hut on Peak-of-the-gods. He had poked around his home and had easily come upon the damning evidence... Baju's well-read Bible. Confiscating the book, he had ordered Baju to follow him to the police station.

In those days, a policeman seldom, if ever, carried a gun. The villagers always felt so intimidated that the symbolic little stick they carried was sufficient to reinforce their power and establish their will. In fact, in these remote parts the lowliest policeman was king. So it really irritated Baju that this policeman had come carrying a pistol. It was as if he, a cripple, was some sort of dangerous criminal.

Baju had protested about leaving his home right then. Everyone else in the family was gone—out in the jungle herding cows, collecting firewood, or working in some distant field. His job that day was to look after the house and his little grandson. But the policeman's job was to arrest him and bring him in. So abandoning the toddler who was crying out for him from the doorway, Baju started down the mountain.

From the streambed at the bottom of the gorge up to Dhobadi was a climb of nearly 4,000 feet. "*Kentek, ken-tek, ken-tek,*" up the mountain they toiled. Baju was in turmoil now as thoughts churned through his mind. What was he going to say? How could he answer their questions? Then halfway to the top, God spoke to him.

It seemed as if Baju never tired of reading his Bible. Reading two, three, or four hours a day was his norm. He was a slow reader and he carefully pondered the meaning of each passage and how it applied to him. This day, Jesus' words came to him and he remembered the whole passage clearly:

> *"On my account you will be brought before governors and kings as witnesses to them and to the Gentiles. But when they arrest you, do not worry about what to say or how to say it. At that time you will be given what to say, for it will not be you speaking, but the Spirit of your Father speaking through you,"* (Matthew 10:18-20).

It all became so apparent now, and peace flooded his heart and mind. If he were brought before the Governor, it wouldn't be the witchdoctor who did it. Neither would it be the police. It would be Jesus who had sent him there as a witness. This situation was all about the Kingdom of God. Consequently, his trials would be under God's control, and by no means should he worry about the outcome. But most importantly, he should not make any plans about what to say. That might only interfere with what the Holy Spirit wanted to speak through him. Why worry? God had promised to work it out for good, both for him, as well as for me. And... that is how it all happened.

Sitting in the jail cell, Baju did not feel the least bit intimidated. Furthermore, the police did not mistreat him. Probably they felt too ashamed to beat such an old soldier, and a cripple at that. Yes, it was cold up there and the food was pretty poor. When they did bring him food, the rice was the blackened scrapings from the bottom of the pot. Nevertheless, as usual, Baju gave thanks to God for what was given to him. But that was not all. He used that opportunity to thank God and bless the policemen as well. This was so strange to the guard that he yelled out across the yard to his companions, "Hey, he is praying for us!"

The following day, Baju's wife came up to the police station. She was distraught. What would she do without him? All she seemed to do was cry and tell him to obey the police. Just do whatever was necessary to get out of jail. That, of course, would be to give a bribe and recant his allegiance to Jesus. This was unthinkable to a great sinner like Baju. Meanwhile, he had noticed that Kissery was in pain and limping. So before she left, Baju prayed for her leg and it was healed. She returned down the mountain walking well, but she was not at all consoled by her husband's stubbornness.

After thirteen days and no bribe forthcoming, the policemen took Baju down the mountain and off to the District Headquarters. There, the district governor would decide what to do with him. The law was clear: One could be sentenced for three years in prison for changing his religion, and another three years if you had influenced someone else to do likewise. Baju was fully and genuinely guilty on both counts. His guilt, however, did nothing to diminish the peace of God that prevailed in his heart.

When he was brought before the Governor, it must have been an interesting sight. The Governor would have been a college graduate. Baju, on the other hand, had never been to a formal school. He stood there before the governor's desk, an old soldier at attention, propped up by two home-made bamboo crutches. What would Baju say? Or rather, what would God have to say?

The Governor looked at the charge sheet and then asked Baju directly, "Are you a Christian?"

Without hesitation and with a strong voice Baju answered, "Yes, sir!"

One might imagine the surprise of the Governor when Baju immediately confessed to his crime. Thieves, murderers, and criminals of all types were frequently brought before him. All of them would have either denied the charges or have had some grand excuse or mitigating circumstances to relate. But not Baju. He must have appeared so ignorant. He had confessed to his crime without any apparent thought about its ramifications. At his age, already some 30 years past the average lifespan for his people, it was very likely that he could die in prison.

Puzzled by this strange old man, the Governor asked, "Why?"

And there it was, just as Jesus had promised. The answer from the Spirit came from Baju's heart so calmly, so truthfully, so simply: "Sir, I heard it. I liked it. I embraced it."

Dumbfounded, and maybe a little exasperated or amused, the Governor might have thought how ignorant, how stupid can you get? What harm can a simple old man like this be? "Go back home," he told Baju, "and do whatever you want to do."

If the Governor were just being compassionate, one could imagine him turning Baju loose only on the condition that he didn't talk to others about Jesus. But instead, there were no restrictions. No reprimand. Nothing.

Under normal circumstances in those days, prisoners seldom left the police station, much less the district prison without paying a hefty bribe. Baju could have arranged that payoff while he was in jail in Dhobadi, and he supposed that was the reason they had kept him there so long. But giving a bribe was an anathema to him. He would rather rot in prison. That being the case, the villagers were amazed when two days later Baju suddenly showed up. Having been sent before the Governor, they didn't expect to see him for a long time, if ever again.

—Postscript—

Some years later, we brought Baju to the U.S. At that time he had many opportunities to speak at various meetings. It was then that Baju's experience gave me no small difficulty.

The grammar of Magar is such that the verb is usually the last word in a sentence. And not unusually, the verb at the very end of a paragraph is what makes the whole discourse fit together. So if I didn't happen to be familiar with the story he was telling, I wouldn't know how to translate it for him into English. Then I would have a real struggle maintaining the story flow, because the key word that everything turned on might only come at the very end.

Consequently, I would sometimes ask him what he was planning to speak about at the meeting. His answer was always the same: "I don't know."

Sometimes I would prod him to consider some story or experience. Or I would try to pry out of him what he might have been thinking about recently. But he was immoveable. If I persisted, he would remind me that the Matthew scripture said, *"Don't even think about what you are going to say, for the Spirit will speak through you."*

It didn't matter to him that Jesus was referring to the times when you are face to face with governors and kings. It didn't matter that this had to do with when you were on trial. For Baju, if Jesus said not to worry and not to think about your answer, then he was good with that. He would do it... all the time.

As a result, though I sometimes had difficulty in translating smoothly for him, it seemed that Baju was right, for people were greatly blessed. God's Spirit always spoke through him, just as he expected.

CHAPTER 24

THE TEARS

"A woman who had lived a sinful life...
stood behind him at his feet weeping..."
Luke 7:37-38

Suddenly Baju began sobbing uncontrollably. When he finally recovered his composure, all that he could say was, *"jammai, jammai."*

"All," I inquired?

"Yes," he replied, "all of them! I've done them ALL!!!"

It was probably the winter of 1981, and Baju and I had been working on passages such as: *"The acts of the sinful nature are obvious: sexual immorality, impurity and debauchery; idolatry and witchcraft; hatred, discord, jealousy, fits of rage, selfish ambition, dissensions, factions and envy; drunkenness, orgies and the like,"* (Galatians 5:19-21).

All the sins the scriptures speak of — Baju had done them all! He had told me of incidents like the time when someone's goat had wandered by and he had killed and eaten it. He had also alluded to some terrible things that occurred while he was in the British Gurkha Forces fighting rebels along the Afghanistan border from 1935 to 1937. I had known that all his life he had been an enthusiastic reprobate, but it seemed a bit far-fetched to say that he had done everything. Nevertheless, that is how he perceived it, and I never asked for more detail.

Baju was 61 years old when he began to work for us, and he became a follower of Jesus within a month. Now, as we worked over the translation, he was reminded of the many evils in which he had so eagerly once participated. The result: great sobbing tears of shame and sorrow.

Baju, the derelict, was a perfect example of Jesus' teaching to Simon the Pharisee: *"Therefore, I tell you, her many sins have been forgiven—for she loved much. But, he who has been forgiven little, loves little,"* (Luke 7:47).

The gratefulness Baju felt for knowing that his past was washed away by the blood of Jesus had no bounds, and henceforth he lived a life of joy. It produced a love that propelled him across the rugged mountains, despite an aging body and the loss of a leg. The persecution and the Witchdoctor's constant threats did nothing to dampen his love. It was a love that had to be shared. Many others recanted their faith, but not him. An unimaginably great price had been paid for his freedom, and free he would always be.

—Postscript—

Baju was very concerned that he obeyed Jesus completely. Consequently, among other things, he did not avoid dealing with the sin of a judgmental spirit. He knew it crippled spiritual growth and would steal his joy. Unlike us in America, he would not try to get around it by calling it *constructive criticism.*

The Magars have the perfect parallel to Jesus' teaching of the "speck in your brother's eye" (Matthew 7:3-5). Of such a person they say, *"He spots the louse crawling on his brother's back, but he can't see the water buffalo walking on his own back."*

Baju had seen the buffalo and had left it at the foot of the Cross. He wouldn't be fussed by the lice he saw crawling on others. He had been freed from sin, and the joy of the Lord was his strength. This day, however, he had glanced back at that enormous *water buffalo* which had once owned him. It loosed a shame and sorrow that had rushed upon him and for just this moment, his normally joyful demeanor had been overwhelmed.

CHAPTER 25

THE BEGGAR BOY

It was the summer of 1985, and we were living up in Jawalakhel in Kathmandu. Meena, who had been our faithful house helper since 1970, had finally decided to follow Jesus... largely due to Baju's continued encouragement.

I had obtained a short contract with Save the Children (Norway) to implement a community development project for the remote mountain region west of Arakhala. This provided us a resident visa, as well as an opportunity to get to know a huge Magar population I had never contacted before. Additionally, it paid rent on a large house and gave us a salary sufficient to hire a cook.

Persecution of Christians was intense in those days, so we were particularly careful about what we said to Nepali nationals. We had hired Haree to do the daily shopping and cooking for us so that we could host more company. Our missionary friends and acquaintances appreciated Haree's excellent meals and our home became a bit of an oasis for many. Also, we could now house and conveniently feed the Magars who came in from the villages with serious medical needs.

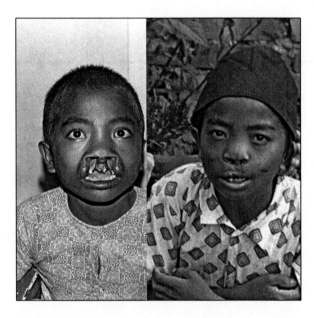

A cleft lip village boy — before and after

Haree, a quick tempered young man, was known to tear up Bibles until he himself became a believer. Now, he was just as quick and bold to tell others about Jesus. Between Meena and Haree, the Good News was shared from the back door of our kitchen on a regular basis. Among other things, it was Meena or Haree's job to attend to the regular stream of beggars that rattled our gate. They were to give them a cup of tea sloshing with sugar and a piece of bread slathered high with peanut butter. This extra bit of generosity would sometimes provide an opportunity to share something about Jesus with people who had never before heard of the Name.

One day, Meena came to me because she was puzzled over the requests of a young beggar. I went out to find a boy about twelve years old sitting on the ground. I don't remember if he had asked specifically for anything. I do remember, however, that he didn't want sugar in his tea and he didn't want this or that. Strange behavior, for a beggar.

A month earlier he had been brought into Kathmandu by an uncle who had left him at the government hospital. He had just been discharged and was about to begin a twelve-day trek back home by himself. He didn't know what disease he had. But he had been instructed that when he arrived home he was to go immediately to the Okhaldhunga Mission Hospital to get more medicine.

The Swiss were building a road out East and I knew that traffic had already begun moving on it. So I wondered why it would take him so long to get back home. It turned out that his uncle had left him with no money, probably assuming that it was just his karma to die there anyway. We asked for his medical reports and with no small effort managed to decipher that he was suffering from diabetes.

We calculated that if he took a bus to the end of the road, he could make it over the mountains to his home in about five days. We gave him enough money to cover his bus fare, as well as to buy his meals along the way. If he hadn't come to our gate that day, and if God hadn't given us the patience to search out his problem, I wonder how he would have had the strength to make it home alive.

"Give to the one who asks you, and do not turn away from the one who wants to borrow from you."
Matthew 5:42

CHAPTER 26

THE PROPHECY

Baju was about as upset as he could get. Once again the power of the witchdoctors had triumphed. A woman, one of his relatives, had just died from a curse.

The village of Chuli Bojha, about two hours up the mountain from Arakhala, had been famous for their powerful witchdoctors. Years before, through the power of his guiding spirits, one the witchdoctors, had prophesied that his own daughter would die at the age of forty.

When we first came to Nepal, the average life expectancy was thirty-nine years, and I surmised that in these poor Magar villages it must have been somewhat less. So to die at age forty would not be so bad, unless you were that girl who had been cursed. As it happened, she married a fellow from Arakhala and went about life just as everyone else. But at the age of forty she got very sick. She was a relative by marriage to Baju, so he went to visit her. After Baju prayed for her, she recovered. However, a couple of months later she became sick again. So Baju returned to her house, and again she was healed.

During the monsoon season we used to move back to Kathmandu and work there on language projects. Baju would come also and live with us there for two or three months at a time. On this occasion, when he returned home to Arakhala, he learned that the lady had gotten sick again and that she had died... at age forty. This was not the first time that this sort of incident had occurred, but it always disappointed him markedly. He had endured constant persecution at the hands of the witchdoctors, yet he had always overcome. The villagers had seen innumerable healings in the Name of Jesus, yet they could not break free of the witchdoctors' controlling influence. They were just too fearful of their spirit power.

Thinking back on those seventeen years that Baju was the only follower of Jesus in Arakhala reminds me of how much his situation and his life paralleled that of the prophet Jeremiah. And like Jeremiah, he too stood unflinchingly against the enemies of God. Yet at the same time, Baju cared for them deeply, just as the Father instructed. God gave Jeremiah strict instructions about compromising his message, and Baju readily followed that pattern.

"Let this people turn to you,
But you must not turn to them.
I will make you a wall to this people,
A fortified wall of bronze;
They will fight against you

But will not overcome you,
For I am with you
To rescue and save you.
I will save you from the hands of the wicked
And redeem you from the grasp of the
*   cruel."*
Jeremiah 15:19-21

Another incident happened in regard to the village of Charcharya. This was the home village of Baju's first wife, which was located three rugged valleys to the east. Baju had close drinking buddies there and maintained a good relationship with the leaders, who were his in-laws. At least once, and sometimes twice a year, he would pick up his crutches and set out across the mountains to visit them. It seemed that he could not keep the Good News a secret. He himself was a chief of sinners, and God's forgiveness for sinners such as himself was always close to his heart. Despite the good relationships he had in Charcharya, and despite the demonstration of God's healing power among them, Baju never found a single person who would ask God to forgive them of their sins.

Perhaps the Hindu concept of karma had done its work too thoroughly. In Hinduism, it seems that forgiveness from God could not be obtained through repentance. Instead, today's sins were to be paid for in the next reincarnation and one could do little to change his karma in this life. One's only hope was to counter-balance the effect of his sin in a future life by doing many good deeds in this life.

One day Baju came back from Charcharya and told me that he would not return to that village ever again. And to my remembrance, he never did. They would not turn from their ways. He had had a heart-to-heart talk with his relative, the village leader, and the man had made it clear that on no account would they change their ways. They had made their choice. There was nothing more that Baju could do.

Not many months later, tragedy struck in Charcharya. As sometimes happens, a gust of wind blew a flame of fire up to the very low ceiling in one of those houses. After months and years the smoke builds up around cobwebs into long tendrils which dangle from the ceilings above the fire. I suppose that it was one of those hanging tendrils that caught fire. It was the middle of the day and only a few old ladies were still in the village.

Traditionally, Magar houses are packed very closely together. In fact, it was not unusual to overhear a conversation in your neighbor's house. Charcharya Village was built in a tight little bowl right below the pass, and once one house caught fire, the wind storm, which swirled around and around, carried the wild flames from one thatched roof to the next. In the end, all forty houses were burnt to the ground and everything was lost. Baju was not at all surprised. After years of sacrificial effort on his part, they had rejected God outright. Consequently, God had pulled back the angels which had guarded their village from Satan's outright assault. And so, the enemy had come in like a flood.

*"We know that we are the children of God,
and that the whole world is under the
control of the evil one."*
1 John 5:19

—Postscript—

This last story raises a point of theology: Does God allow evil? Baju seemed to understand that Satan hates mankind with a furious rage. If Satan were left unrestricted, all humanity, all those who are made in God's image, would soon be wiped from the earth. Consequently, God has sent angels on assignment to protect all people from quick annihilation. Believers, unbelievers, the good and the evil, are all constantly being protected by God. God's patience, however, does have a limit. There comes a time and place where God relents to mankind's self-will. That is, He will allow men to have their way. When the angels' protective shield is pulled back, to that degree, tragedy and destruction follow close behind.

Woman grinding grain

CHAPTER 27

THE LAST PAGE

We were in desperate need of a dedicated helper... someone we could rely on to help us begin Bible translation. For nearly four years we had been without a faithful language helper. We had hired a number of people, but they had stuck with it for only a short while. In those days, little was known of the grammar and structure of these unwritten Himalayan languages. This meant that it was up to us to discover the unique patterns of Magar.

At the end of May 1973, it looked as if our prayers were answered. Village leaders had assigned someone to be our teacher and he had agreed to live with us in Kathmandu during the monsoon season. This was great news until the man showed up. It was Baju—the man we knew only as a drinker, gambler, and carouser!

Greatly dejected, I asked if another person could somehow be found. But no, Baju was the man. I was certain then that it was just another one of Satan's plans to ruin our work. So I prayed strongly against it. I asked God to let Baju become sick or whatever—just find us someone else. But when the day came for us to leave for Kathmandu, there was Lucifer's agent full of energy and eager to go!

(In those days we were very careful about sharing our faith. We could be reported and expelled from the country. In fact, three years later our project was closed down and we did have to leave.)

When we arrived in Kathmandu, I set a Nepali New Testament out on a table. As Baju was surveying our house, he came across the Book. "May I read this?" he asked.

"If you want to," I replied and suggested he begin with Mark's Gospel.

Before 1950, people from the tribes such as Baju's were not allowed to learn to read and write. That privilege was reserved for the high caste Hindus. Baju, however, had been taught to read Nepali when he became a soldier in the British Gurkha Forces. He could read alright, but just barely. He would sound out each word, syllable by syllable. Then, at the end of the sentence he would go back and do it again, and then again, until he could finally put it together fast enough to make sense of what he had read.

Moving his finger ever so slowly across the page, Baju would read the Book for two or three hours a day. Meanwhile, I was working on Magar grammar and would get together ten or so examples of something I was trying to unravel. Once I got it laid out, I would go over the examples with Baju. That took just a few minutes, and then I would start working up another set. This gave Baju fifteen or twenty minutes to read. As the Bible story progressed, Baju would regularly ask me questions. Since the Nepali Bible didn't indicate the properties of names, his question would often be something like, "Where is Nathanael located?" Or, "Who is Jerusalem?"

After perhaps two-and-a-half weeks, Baju was reaching the end of Mark's Gospel. The living conditions in Bible times were all so familiar to him. He had lived through locust plagues and famines. His relatives had contracted leprosy and were expelled from the village. They had lived alone in the forest where they had died a lonely and pitiful death. Plagues of smallpox, typhoid, and cholera had swept through the villages, taking the lives of young and old. His own Grandfather Aganda, with whom he had lived as a young boy, was the most powerful shaman known in that part of Nepal. Fear and dread of witchcraft, demons, and evil spirits filled the lives of all the villagers.

Into their kind of world came a man named Jesus. He healed the sick and cast out demons. He made the lepers whole and fed the hungry. He gave life to the dead and the greatest of sinners found forgiveness. Without a doubt, this was the Son of God. How wonderful that must have been!

One day as Baju read on, the story turned into a tragedy. The authorities arrested Jesus and gave Him a mock trail. Then they nailed Him to a post—something called a cross. He cried out to Heaven, "My God! My God! Why have you forsaken me?"

God had answered Jesus when He had prayed for others. But when He prayed for Himself, God did not hear. And now, He who gave life to the dead, Himself died in abject agony. Baju thought to himself, "No! No! This can't happen!"

Across the table, Baju was in deep anguish and groaned quietly as this immense travesty unfolded before him. He seemed to take ever so long to work his finger back and forth across the page. Finally reaching the last page he read on. "What is this? He has risen from the grave? He is alive?"

Not many days later I was hospitalized. I had contracted mononucleosis and nearly died of liver failure. As soon as I was strong enough to travel, we returned to the United States. Baju went back to his village where, unknown to us, he threw away his whiskey bottle and began eagerly sharing this Good News.

A year later we returned to Nepal, and in the coming years, a number of people in our village wanted to follow in Jesus' way. They all plainly saw the great change in Baju. He went from a hard drinking old soldier to one who was soft and caring for all. Furthermore, he had no fear whatsoever of the witches, the witchdoctors, or demonic spirits. Jesus had conquered all that darkness. In addition, God declared him who had been a sinner among sinners, to be forgiven. Jesus had promised that He would always be his companion, a friend who would daily be closer to him than a brother.

But the pattern among the villagers was always the same: One after another, they eventually recanted under the witchdoctor's unrelenting pressure and constant threats. For seventeen long years, worship meetings consisted of Baju, Barbara, and me. As the years wore on, I sometimes became discouraged and wondered whether or not our work was worth the sacrifices. But then, I would remember that day I watched Baju read the last page... and once again I would find the encouragement to continue on.

> *"Let us not become weary in doing good,*
> *for at the proper time we will reap a*
> *harvest if we do not give up."*
> Galatians 6:9

Michael plowing, Adina planting corn seed

CHAPTER 28

THE BUS TRIP

"Because he loves Me," says the
Lord, "I will rescue him."
Psalm 91:14

Some of Baju's favorite verses were in Psalm 91, where God promises to *"command His angels concerning you."* Before a trip, he always asked God to send His angels to protect the vehicle and to put their hands on the driver's hands. In Nepal, that was a particularly good idea. Every week or two we would hear of a vehicle going off the road and plunging into a gorge or a river. Most, if not all, of the passengers were lost or severely injured.

The buses, especially in the earlier years, had already been worn out from years of hard service down in India. We, however, didn't mind their rusty shells, the holes in their floors, nor the cracked and inoperable windows. We were just thankful that we didn't have to walk those many hard miles. What

I didn't like though, was the way the front wheels wobbled when the bus labored up and down the mountain roads. In a Hindu land where fate ruled, repairing something before it was broken seemed rather useless. Nothing bad was going to happen anyway unless it was someone's karma. So why worry?

It would be okay, of course, when a tie rod failed on the inside wheel. The bus would just ram into the side of the mountain—the result of which we regularly saw. But when the tie rod on the outside wheel gave way, the bus would career off the narrow road and over the edge. Only those riding on top would have any chance to jump... and that was why I often preferred riding on the bus' roof with the luggage.

In Baju's case, he had been working with me in Kathmandu and was returning home. By then, the main highway had been widened a bit which helped the flow of traffic. In earlier years there had been room on the asphalt for only one vehicle, so when you met someone coming, one or both of you had to pull onto the shoulder to get by.

Loaded to the gills, Baju's bus was lumbering down the highway towards Mugling. On the right side, many hundreds of feet below, the Trisuli River flowed through the gorge. When the mechanism of their right front wheel gave way, it was the worst case scenario. Thankfully, they weren't going very fast and the brakes on the ancient vehicle had had some effect before it lurched over the side. However, instead of plummeting down the steep slope and into the river, the bus shuddered to a stop. At the very point where it went over the side, there was a tiny road. This temporary track had been scratched out of the mountainside to transport rock and gravel up from the river for a recent upgrade.

Many would say it was luck. Hindus would say it was their karma. Baju, however, was fully convinced that the angels he had requested had not failed in their assignment. They had held the wheel in place until the bus had reached this very point on the road. Then, when the tie rod came apart and the loose wheel yanked the bus off to the right, the angels had shepherded it over the side onto this narrowest of lanes. Everyone got off the bus without incident and transferred to other buses which came along later. It was a non-event. Otherwise, most likely, everyone would have been killed or drowned in the raging river below.

"IF you make the Most High your dwelling...
Then no harm will befall you...
For He will command His angels concerning
you to guard you in all your ways."
Psalm 91:9-11

CHAPTER 29

THE POOP
❧❦❧❦

Baju's attackers were stunned! With three short words they had been rendered speechless.

Some might even say it was a stroke of genius. In fact, it was the matchless wisdom of God, spectacular in its simplicity. For me, this may be one of the shortest, as well as one of the most powerful, speeches I have ever known.

To understand, I first need to explain that, except for our own house, there were no toilets in Arakhala Village. So each morning just before daylight, the villagers had to hurry out to the bamboo thickets or to the edges of terrace walls, which they used as their toilets.

In the 70s and 80s, Kalu, the witchdoctor was incessantly persecuting Baju. If he could not stop him from following Jesus, then he would do his best to humiliate him, or at least make fun of him. He seemed to know that he was persecuting a righteous man, because as long as we were in the village, his actions were very low key. However, let us depart for Kathmandu, and sometimes within the very hour he was back harassing Baju in one way or another.

On two occasions, he gathered up some of his cronies and surrounded Baju while he was resting on the flat rocks under the banyan tree next to our house. In both instances, they carried large sticks with which they threatened to beat him to death if he would not renounce Jesus. Their demand, as usual, was that he join them in their sacrifices to the village gods. And, not unlike what Jesus did at the cliff near Nazareth (Luke 4:28-30), both times Baju bravely walked untouched through the midst of the crowd.

Sacrificing a chicken

During one of those incidents, they were bringing accusations and raving at him. Suddenly the witch-doctor's son demanded, "Bring your Lord right here!" he shouted. "Show us your Lord now! Then we will believe."

Baju was certain that God's Spirit would speak to him in times such as these, so he always listened for that quiet voice in his heart. What came out of his mouth shocked his tormentors. "You poop here!" he retorted, pointing to the ground.

Then he picked up his crutches and made his way through the speechless crowd. With those three words Baju not only *plugged the mouth* of his opponents, he also taught them a deep Bible truth.

First of all, the witchdoctor's son was by no means able to poop on demand. He could strain and push all he wanted, but everyone knew he wouldn't be able to produce anything. Pooping was done in the early morning, not in the evening as it so happened to be. Furthermore, not only was there a right time to poop, there was also the proper place to poop. This was done in seclusion in the dark of the early dawn, not in the midst of a crowd of people.

The villagers had, most likely, heard Baju proclaim that Jesus would return one day. That had probably precipitated this challenge from the witchdoctor's son. But since it was obvious that he himself could not manage a natural bodily function on demand, it was ridiculous to ask Baju to perform a miracle and produce Jesus Christ on demand.

Baju's Lord will certainly return. However, His coming will not be dictated by nature nor by the whims of men. He will return at a time and an hour He is not expected (Matthew 24:44). Furthermore, His return will not be in seclusion or in the presence of a few. His return will be preceded by the trumpet call of God. And it will be like the lightning which flashes and lights up the sky from one end to the other (Luke 18:24).

> *"Behold, I am coming soon! My reward is with me, and I will give to everyone according to what he has done. I am the Alpha and the Omega, the First and the Last, the Beginning and the End."*
> Revelation 22:12-13

—Postscript—

Baju's reply was a powerful rebuttal of the demand to produce the Lord Jesus at that time and place. With Baju's demand that the witchdoctor's son poop "right here," his accusers immediately realized how their demand to produce Jesus was also absurd.

We returned to Dallas in June 1986. The intermittent sicknesses and continued high stresses of living in Nepal had become too much for Barbara and she had become subject to periods of depression. We were in the U.S. until August 1989, at which time Adina went off to college.

—Trials and Miracles—

(1986-1989)

CHAPTER 30

THE UNFULFILLED HOPE

I had been continuing in sin, for sure! The problem was not them, the problem was me. Some, of course, might suggest that it was not all that significant. However, the Word is clear; *"Everything that does not come from faith is sin!"* (Romans 14:23).

On the other hand, what was so bad about trusting one's friends? After all, we had really been close. In our time of need, it seemed right to think that we could count on them. We had given up everything to work in Nepal, while they had stayed at home and had done very well. Whenever we were in the U.S., we would drive quite a distance to see them. They would encourage us and he would never fail to tell me *"Gary, I pray for you every day!"*

It was a bit of a dilemma. We were back in the U.S. and living expenses were more than in Nepal. In earlier years, our finances had been sufficient, but now as our kids got older and the working expenses rose, our needs increased faster than we had acquired additional support. It was our policy, however, to say nothing about our financial situation. If friends did not ask, we did not tell. But these folks topped our list of discerning and committed friends. "Surely," I thought, "with the sort of money they are making, they would want to support us."

And that was my hope. But it never happened. Every time it was the same: With warm enthusiasm they welcomed us, and when we left they would slip us an envelope with a hundred-dollar bill inside.

Money was the last thing I ever wanted to talk about, but with a faith mission, we had no salary. We received only what came in and nothing more. When we were back in the U.S., we needed to make the best use of our limited time and energy to meet the right people. And if anyone was right, I was convinced these were the ones. Nevertheless, they never sent a thing to Wycliffe. This continued to bother me. What was their problem?

The problem, however, was me! After years of disappointment, I ever so slowly began to grasp God's plan. Where was my trust? King David had said it so well: *"Search me, oh God, and know my heart; test me and know my anxious thoughts. See if there is any offensive way in me, and lead me in the way everlasting,"* (Psalm 139:23-24).

God was not testing me for His benefit. The test was for me to see my heart and to know my anxious thoughts. Sometimes we really had to pinch pennies, and for many years we had done without a vacation. Nevertheless, we always had enough. Did I hope in God? Of course! But I had also relied on my own understanding, and I had placed my hopes, if not my expectations, in our dear friends.

If we were to talk it over today, I think we would find that these friends had always planned to send us support. However, every time they tried to do so, they were side-tracked. Why? Because God wanted my vacillating trust to become solidly settled on the Rock alone. God wanted to meet our needs in His own ways, so that I would truly lean on Him alone. Then there would be space in my heart for Him to release all His joy and peace as He became the sole Source of an overflowing hope.

> *"May the God of hope fill you with all joy*
> *and peace as you trust in Him, so that you*
> *may overflow with hope by the power of the*
> *Holy Spirit."*
> Romans 15:13

—Postscript—

To this day our friends support the work in Nepal with prayer, but not with finances. God continues to use them to ensure that my hope and my trust remain on Him alone.

CHAPTER 31

DEAD-ON-ARRIVAL

"You will not fear the terror of night..."
Psalm 91:5

The bullet exploded out of the darkness, followed by an ear-shattering blast. The 165-grain projectile hit me with enough force to have lifted 2,000 pounds one foot into the air.

"Dead-On-Arrival!" That is what Lynn, the emergency room nurse, was fully expecting as she waited for the ambulance to arrive. She had seen gunshot victims before, but never anyone who had been shot through the middle with a large hunting rifle. Those people were usually taken directly to the morgue.

Half an hour after sunset, the end of legal shooting time, Michael and I turned around and started back. In the deepening darkness twenty minutes later, we were walking up a paved road. Unknown to us, two hunters were loading their deer into a pick-up truck seventy-five yards ahead. One hunter glanced up, saw four legs on the dark road and somehow presumed a deer. He grabbed his friend's rifle, took aim, and fired.

Michael was thirteen, and this was my first opportunity to take him deer hunting. Deer had over-populated South Texas and for the nominal fee of one hundred dollars, a rancher had allowed us to harvest four deer each. That added up to a substantial amount of very good meat. Roger and Barb, a couple from church, as well as Barbara, Michael and I, had driven down from Dallas that day. Before dark, we had gone to scout out the land. Roger went one way and Michael and I the other.

The bullet came straight at me, struck my belt, entered my stomach and exploded out the back of my pelvis. The force blew me backwards onto the pavement. I neither felt nor heard a thing. A minute or so later, I regained consciousness and tried to make sense of what seemed like a bit of stinging in my abdomen. When my hand sank into the bloody hole in my back, I realized that I had been shot. Then I knew... I was as good as dead!

Meanwhile, Michael had lain down beside me, not seeing or understanding what had happened in the semi-darkness. When he heard me feebly say, *"I'm shot!"* and saw the blood on my hand, he sprang up and ran for help. About forty yards up the road he yelled out. Soon the hunter and two boys were at my side, weeping uncontrollably. The unthinkable had happened—he had killed a man.

Michael stopped the second hunter from running down to watch me die and instructed him to bring their pickup truck. Loading me into the front seat, they raced for help while Michael filled the bloody hole in my back with paper napkins.

While I had been lying on the pavement, God did three things: First, He gave me an indescribable peace—not an assurance that I wouldn't die, but that live or die, all was well. Secondly, He gave me the words, "The blood of Jesus," to speak over and over. This simple prayer proclaimed Jesus' victory over all of Satan's plans. When my body was as good as dead, my spirit rose up strong. I refused to passively acquiesce to the inevitable, if God had another plan. Thirdly, despite the increasing pain, He gave me a crystal clear mind to direct the traumatized hunters in rescuing me.

I had shot deer and a moose before and had no illusions. I knew I would die. If I were to survive, it would be an act of God and God alone. Since the shock power of the bullet had failed to kill me outright—no small miracle in itself—the immediate danger was bleeding to death. Twenty minutes later, we were at the medical facility in Junction. By God's providence, just as my veins began collapsing a medic got a needle into my left hand and started an intravenous drip. Seconds later, my veins did collapse and, try as he would, he was unable to get a needle into my other hand.

"My blood type is O positive," I told him, and the medics started pouring blood into me—eight units in all before the night was over.

Earlier, when the pickup had reached the gate of the ranch, I had told Michael to jump out and run to tell Barbara what had happened. Expecting my wife and friends to soon find us, I instructed the medic to have Roger come in to see me when they arrived. "Tell him to bring a pencil and paper," I said. But by the time Roger got there, I was so weak that I could speak only one word at a time. I knew if I were to survive by some great miracle, it would be because of prayer. So Roger leaned his ear close to my mouth and wrote. Little by little, I managed to whisper six names in six cities. At that point Roger stopped my struggle. He knew I wouldn't make it. With eyes full of tears, he squeezed my shoulder, promised he would look after Michael, and went out.

For her part, Barbara had phoned our Wycliffe friend, Marj Warkentin in Dallas. But then, the realization began to sink in and when she reached her parents in San Diego, she was unable to speak. She gave the phone to Michael who explained to his grandparents what had happened. They belonged to Skyline, a large active church. Immediately, the call went out on the Wycliffe prayer chain in Dallas, as well as the Skyline prayer chain. In addition, Roger had reached four of the whispered names, and the call for prayer was going out from those points as well. So even before we left Junction, a large number of people were already standing in the gap for us.

Everyone who saw me knew I couldn't survive. Everyone but one. I found out later that only Michael knew differently. He knew that I couldn't die. He had seen God do great things in Nepal and it didn't seem at all strange to him that God would once again intervene with a miracle. After all, he reasoned, Dad hadn't finished the work yet. He was certain that God's plan was for the Magar people to have a New Testament. Since it wasn't completed, Dad's work on earth wasn't done.

They could do little for me in Junction, so after emergency treatment I was put into an ambulance and sent to the regional hospital, fifty-five miles away down Interstate Highway 10. As we raced down the freeway, I heard the driver repeatedly questioning the medic attending me. He knew what was inevitable.

When we arrived in Kerrville, the surgeons sliced me open from top to bottom, removed eight inches of colon and cleaned up the mess as best they could. Later, the surgeon exclaimed what a miracle it was: Had the course of the bullet been altered by even the slightest degree it would have ripped open a large vein, an artery, or an organ. That would have brought about a quick death.

A week after the accident, with my right leg mostly paralyzed, I asked the orthopedic surgeon for a prognosis. He assured me that I wouldn't be confined to a wheelchair, but I would need some support to walk again. I had a fifty percent chance of walking with a walker and an equal chance of eventually walking with only a cane.

The prayers of many people around the world resulted in my recovering so rapidly that it amazed the surgeon. He sent me home after only two weeks. In Dallas, after three treatments, the physical therapist exclaimed to me, "You've got God in on this!"

A month after the shooting, I graduated from a walker to a cane and even began to walk some without it. Still, I had a fair amount of pain and was very weak. Since the danger of bone infection remained, I continued on high doses of antibiotics.

Celebrations of Christmas, our twenty-second wedding anniversary, and New Year's all took a back seat as we basked in the gift of life given to us in Jesus' powerful name. The great and mighty promises of Psalm 91, which David Watters and I had tested when we traversed the Himalayas eighteen years earlier, had once again proven faithful and true:

> *"You will not fear the terror of night,*
> *nor the arrow that flies by day...*
>
> *If you make the Most High your dwelling—*
> *even the Lord, who is my refuge—*
> *then no harm will befall you...*
>
> *For he will command his angels concerning*
> *you to guard you in all your ways...*
>
> *'Because he loves Me,' says the Lord,*
> *'I will rescue him;*
>
> *I will protect him, for he acknowledges My*
> *name.*
> *He will call upon Me, and I will answer him;*
>
> *I will be with him in trouble,*
> *I will deliver him...'"*
>   Psalm 91:5, 9-15

—Postscript—

There are two Rogers in this story. Roger Fry, my friend from church, who came with his wife Barb and my wife Barbara. The second Roger, who shot me, was hunting with his friend and their two young sons. We had never met them before. A few weeks after the shooting accident, we invited Roger and his wife to our home. We assured them that he was forgiven and that we would not sue them. Furthermore, I would not press criminal charges, which would probably have resulted in jail time for Roger. I told him that just as Jesus had set me free, so too, I was now setting him free.

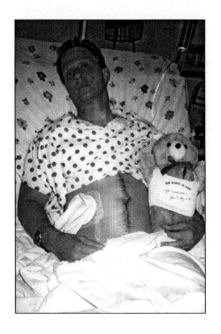

Gary in hospital

CHAPTER 32

THE EXPLOSION

❧❧❧

*"The thief comes only to steal and
kill and destroy..."*
John 10:10

All we wanted to do was to recover our health
and return to Nepal. But death was lurking
in our peaceful backyard that spring day in March
1988.

The job was supposed to have been rather
simple—just replace two rotted fence posts. After
being shot through the middle four months earlier, my
overall strength was returning despite the continuing
atrophy of my right leg. When I needed to walk, my
cane kept me steady, which made this small project
doable. Besides, it would save us money.

The problem arose when I discovered that the
original posts had been set in concrete. I had been
unable to break up the cement, so I began to dig
a new hole next to the old one. For this job, I had

borrowed an all-steel clamshell type posthole digger. As I slowly worked the new hole deeper, I began to run into pieces of brick and sticks that were buried when the house lot had been leveled. The heavy steel blades worked well to cut through the junk until I hit a particularly tough piece at the side of the hole about eighteen inches down.

Unable to get past it, I got down on my hands and knees and tried digging with my steel crowbar. The problem was compounded by the fact that I couldn't see into that dark hole very well. I wanted to go just six inches deeper to make sure the fence didn't fall over again anytime soon. But when I was unable to get that thick piece of plastic out with the crowbar, it was back to the heavy posthole digger.

Spreading my feet a bit farther apart, so I wouldn't lose balance and slash my foot, I lifted the steel handles as high as I dared and slammed it down into the hole. Failing to cut through, I tried again, lifting higher... but to no avail. Trying yet again, I put all my weight into it.

Kaaaboom!! A six-inch wide column of fire leapt from the hole, stopping just short of my nose! This was the first very loud noise I had experienced since that rifle blast had knocked me down. Frozen, I stood there in shock... my strength completely drained. Down the street a neighbor opened his door and yelled out, "What's going on out there!"

I was completely mystified. How, I wondered, could a grenade or a stick of dynamite have gotten buried in my backyard in Dallas?

It took quite some time to pull myself together. Knocking weakly on my neighbor's door, he told me that a few minutes earlier his lights had dimmed. Indeed, hidden behind our fence, less than twenty feet away was a transformer. I had struck the 200-ampere, 240-volt underground wires that serviced his house. Later investigation showed that the fence builder had simply set the original post right on top of the wire.

When I retrieved the posthole digger, it had two pencil-size holes in the steel blade. The electric surge had simply vaporized the steel! My mighty push had been sufficient to cut the heavy plastic insulation in such a way that one blade had contacted both wires simultaneously. This had saved my life. Piercing only one wire could have brought 200 amperes up one arm, through my heart and into the other arm which was grasping the steel handle. Fatal!

A number of people had told me that Satan didn't want the Magar New Testament finished. Yet after every sickness and multiple setbacks, we regrouped and forged on. For years we had known that under the conditions that existed then in Nepal, it would be impossible to complete the work. Consequently we would aim for the possible... translate just one book at a time. In this way, the first draft of the New Testament had been completed in 1982. By 1988, many checks and numerous revisions had been completed. With things shaping up, the final goal was coming into sight. I had heard of Satan's attacks on folks who were trying to finish a New Testament.

But after all, having come this far, one doesn't easily turn back from the call.

In hindsight, I understand the extent of that opposition more clearly. Barbara had begun wilting under periods of depression, requiring us to return to Dallas in June 1986. In November 1987, I survived a bullet that had the power to lift 2,000 pounds one foot into the air. Now again, in March 1988, I was nearly electrocuted. How could I even imagine that before we would see our dear Magar people again, I would face one more test... a King Cobra.

—Comment—

Since it was not sure if, or when, I would ever be strong enough to return to Nepal, we arranged to have Baju come to America. Friends helped us convert our garage in Dallas into a small apartment where he could stay. In this manner we were able to continue our work together. Baju stayed with us for six months in 1988.

CHAPTER 33

THE UNANSWERED PRAYER

"*Mahola. Mahola,*" Baju muttered as I drove toward Kerrville that morning. It was the first Sunday in November of 1988. I had last been on this freeway twelve months earlier riding in the back of an ambulance, with everyone knowing I wouldn't survive. We had been racing through the darkness then, the medic pouring blood into me as fast as he could.

Today, however, I was relaxed and enjoying the scenery. In the back of our beat-up old blue Mazda pickup was a nice eight-point whitetail buck that Baju had shot the day before. We were on our way to speak at a little church. The previous November the folks there had looked after Barbara as I lay dying... and then miraculously recovering in the hospital.

Since we were unable to return to Nepal, friends had managed to get old Baju a passport and onto a flight to America. In Dallas, we were continuing the arduous task of checking and revising, again and again, the Magar New Testament manuscript.

After I had been shot and even after it became apparent that I would indeed walk, I had assumed that I would never hunt again. Some months later it occurred to me that this idea was the world's wisdom... the way of fear. Fear was the exact opposite of faith in our loving Father. So in September, when a friend in church had asked if Baju and I would like to go deer hunting, I had answered, "For sure!"

Baju himself had stepped on a landmine and yet had miraculously survived. That was in 1937, when as a British Gurkha soldier they had been fighting local rebels near the Afghanistan border. His British officer had begged the surgeon to save Baju's arm and he had. But his leg was a different story. Gangrene had set in, and after the third operation his left leg was completely gone.

After three years of living in despondency back at home, Baju decided to get on with life. One day when the village men were going hunting, he picked up his crutches and went along with them. He had an old double-barreled muzzle loader, and over the years he had shot wild boar and even a Bengal tiger. Now he was seventy-six years old, and it had been fifty years since he had handled a rifle. We went out to target practice beforehand, but after he hit the target on his second shot, he absolutely refused to shoot again. Gun powder was expensive in Nepal.

So it was that my friend James Ramsey had taken Baju with him on the opening day of hunting season, and he had shot this nice buck. There were twelve of us hunting on that South Texas ranch, and Baju was the only one to get a deer that day. In another hour, Baju was scheduled to speak in church, and I would translate for him. But his mind obviously wasn't on that. He was gravely concerned over something and he was muttering to himself, "Not enough! Not enough!"

Puzzled, I asked, "What's not enough, Baju?"

"Well, yesterday I asked God for a ten-point buck, but I shot an eight-point instead. Either I was too greedy in asking God for such a big deer, or else a larger one in the woods was coming along soon and I was just too impatient! Was I greedy or impatient?"

I reminded him that among twelve seasoned hunters he was the only one to shoot a deer that day, and it was a nice one at that. He scoffed in a kindly sort of way. That meant nothing. It was no surprise to him that they didn't get one. "They didn't ask God!" he retorted.

It took me some time to understand why Baju was so deeply concerned. Persecution of Christians in Nepal was still continuing. Twice the witchdoctor and his cronies had surrounded Baju, threatening to beat him to death. He was constantly hounded and once jailed for becoming a Christian. It was now fifteen long years that he had been the sole follower of Jesus in Arakhala. Daily he was the object of scorn, criticism, and black magic.

Baju had to know his Father God... or else recant, like so many others before. He had to know his Father's heart. He had to know his Father's will and his Father's voice. Jesus had stated, *"My sheep listen to my voice,"* (John 10:27). Baju, a sheep in God's pasture, was intent on clearly hearing his Shepherd's voice.

He knew his Father's loving heart well, and he would have nothing to do with excuses or explanations. There was no question about why he didn't shoot a ten-point buck. The responsibility was his and his alone. His prayer was unanswered and this was deadly serious. Either he had been impatient or he had been greedy. Whichever it was, he was set on making the correction immediately. For him, hearing God's voice clearly could one day mean the difference between life and death!

CHAPTER 34

ACCORDING TO HIS RICHES

*"And my God will supply all your needs
according to His glorious riches in
Christ Jesus."*
Philippians 4:19

The first time we took Baju deer hunting, Michael was at a football game where he was playing trumpet in the Duncanville High School band. Now it was the first week of December 1988. Football season was over, and Baju was due to return to Nepal in a few days.

Our friend James Ramsey had invited us to hunt one last time at the same ranch we had hunted on four weeks earlier. It was a long drive to South Texas, and we reached the ranch after midnight. We jumped out of bed at 5:30 a.m. and quickly got ready to go. Before we left, however, I asked Baju to pray.

When time was not pressing and things were on his heart, Baju loved to pray on and on, going around the world and back again. But when there was a specific request, he gave thanks to God, got right to the point, and closed by giving thanks again.

So Baju simply asked, "Lord, give us each a deer," and we left. James took Baju, and Michael went with me. Michael had never shot a deer before. The last time he had gone hunting, I had been shot in the dark by another hunter, who didn't know that anybody else was around.

Dawn broke as we waited quietly... a great time to enjoy God's creation. Nothing showed up for a while. Then a small deer came by, but Michael let it pass, hoping for a larger one. Michael was watching in one direction, while I looked in the other. Then, as so often happens, I glanced back to my side and there, a deer had suddenly appeared. When Michael saw the buck, he could hardly believe his opportunity had arrived. He aimed carefully and squeezed the trigger, but his rifle wouldn't fire. When we looked it over, we found that the safety was still on.

Michael aimed again, but this time his rifle was shaking. Hunters call it *buck fever*. I had taught Michael to lock tightly onto the target and wait until he was completely still before pulling the trigger. Only then could he be sure of making a clean kill. The buck was feeding in a narrow clearing 125 yards away. Just one jump and he would be gone from sight. The deer turned away then, and he didn't have a clean shot. So letting up on the trigger, he raised his head and tried to relax.

Soon the deer turned broadside again and he pulled down on it. Watching his rifle barrel shake, I figured this would be pure luck. As much as Michael wanted a deer, however, he found the patience to hold his fire. Again the deer turned away. This scenario happened three times while I wondered when the deer would just disappear into the trees. On the fourth time, however, his barrel finally steadied and squeezing the trigger ever so slowly the rifle fired. He had his first deer! It was even larger than the buck Baju had gotten a month earlier.

After lunch everyone took a nap except Michael, who was too excited to rest. That afternoon we went out to hunt again, but after a short time Michael got tired and wanted to leave. I was hoping to get more of this excellent meat for the freezer. But I couldn't convince him to wait any longer, and we returned to our old Mazda pickup.

As we were driving slowly across the ranch, a few hundred yards ahead of us a herd of deer ran across the road. When we got up there, one deer was still standing at the very edge of the woods. To my astonishment, it just stood there while I took out my rifle and shot it. Shortly after recovering the deer, James drove up. "Come. Bring your pickup and get Baju's deer."

Precisely as Baju had prayed, we had each shot a deer. We weren't pressed to get back to Dallas, so before leaving the next morning, I asked Michael if he wanted to try for another deer and he did. At dawn the next day we were back at the same place and he got one. When we returned to camp with Michael's second deer, I asked Baju what he thought about it. He had asked God for just three deer, but now we had gotten four. I never knew Baju to be confused by a question such as this. He knew God's heart was to *"do exceedingly abundantly above all that we ask or think..."*(Ephesians 3:20). His Father gave *"according to His glorious riches,"* not according to our earthly requests or needs. A great smile came across his face and without hesitation, he replied, "Oh, God is like that. He likes to give us extras!"

CHAPTER 35

THE KING COBRA
❧❦❧

"Because he loves Me," says the Lord,
"I will rescue him."
Psalm 91:14

It was August of 1989, and I had pretty much recovered from the gunshot wound. Barbara was doing much better and now we could return to Nepal to continue our work of revising and checking the Magar New Testament manuscript. Adina had just graduated from High School and was going off to college. Michael was going to Malaysia where he would begin tenth grade. En route from Dallas we had stopped off in Seattle to visit friends and supporters. When we learned that Barbara's mother wasn't doing well, Barbara flew down to San Diego to help her parents while Michael and I went on.

We arrived at the Dalat Boarding School in Penang two days before school started. The next day someone had the great idea to escape the oppressive heat and go for a swim in a water reservoir above the town. So Steve, a school teacher, took me and about ten kids up to the reservoir to swim.

After a half-hour walk through a residential area, we reached the edge of the jungle and started up the hill. We have deadly snakes in Nepal, and during the hot season I am very careful where I step. I had no idea what snakes might inhabit Penang Island, but the dense grass overhanging this narrow path gave me the feeling that it was an ideal habitat for them. So I asked Steve what the situation was with snakes on the island. He assured me not to worry. He had never seen one in the six years that he had lived there.

It was a refreshing time swimming in the deep, cool water. Nevertheless, I was feeling a bit nervous, and I looked very carefully every time I climbed up on a grass-covered rock. This was a new country to me, and I didn't want to get tangled up with a snake.

Then it was time to go. Steve wanted a head start since, he said, the kids would run down the mountain and overtake us. Huge rubber trees overshadowed us as we wandered down the narrow path. Although I had never seen rubber trees before, I recognized them because of the cuts on their trunks. When I remarked to Steve about them, he was surprised to learn that they were rubber trees. That statement should have been my clue...

I was thoroughly enjoying the new jungle sights as I ambled along, wearing the usual rubber flip-flops. Then for no reason at all, I stopped dead still. Looking down, I saw a black snake writhing between my feet!!! Time went into slow motion as I ascended upwards, my eyes fixated incredulously upon the snake. It seemed as if I became suspended in the air, my feet pulled tightly behind my ears. When the snake had slithered off, I put my feet back down on the trail.

Then, from behind me I heard Steve exclaim, *"Woooo! King Cobra!!!"*

When we got back to the school, I went straight to the science room where I found snakes in large glass bottles along with informational displays. A King Cobra's victim was reported to have thirty minutes to get an anti-venom injection or else he was dead!

My left foot had pinned down the cobra's neck in such a manner that he could not turn back and bite me. Stopping as I did, my right foot held the main body down. Had I continued forward, he could have bitten one foot or the other. By ascending straight up, I had probably done the only thing possible to escape being bitten. Why I stopped, how I jumped so high, and how I stayed there until the snake had scurried away, I have no idea.

And so, opposition to the translation work was thwarted by the prayers of our supporters and the promise of our Lord to rescue those who love Him. Psalm 91, which encouraged David Watters and me when we crossed the Himalayas twenty years earlier, makes a direct comment about such things:

"For He will command His angels concerning you to guard you in all your ways...
You will tread upon** the lion and **the cobra..."
'Because he loves Me,' says the Lord,

*'I will rescue him. I will protect him, for he
acknowledges My Name...'*
Psalm 91:11, 13-14

—Postscript—

In the months after I had been shot I marveled at the fact that I was still alive. As time went on, I often wondered what had qualified someone like me to be blessed by such a series of miracles. I was just an ordinary guy, and I certainly had my share of imperfections.

One day, however, I found the answer in Psalm 91:14. *"Because he loves Me," says the Lord, "therefore I will rescue him."* I didn't have to be particularly gifted, and I didn't have to be a saint to qualify. I only needed to love the Lord. That, I knew, I surely did. And so, unknowingly, I had been pre-qualified to receive God's special attention.

—Finishing—

(1989-1990)

CHAPTER 36

THE BEATING
❧❧❧

In our early years in Arakhala, friends used to ask if we had running water in the village. Yes, I assured them; we could get up in the morning and run down the steep 500 foot descent to the spring below Arakhala. There we could find *running* water!

This water emerged out of a rocky hillside at the base of two giant kapok trees. Above these trees, the original covering of deep virgin forest had been clear-cut by Baju's grandfather. There they had planted a little corn and millet. In the following years, continuous erosion had carried away the lush black topsoil and the rocky remains had eventually been left to revert to scrubby brush land. It was on this hillside above the village spring that the beating occurred.

In his waning years, Baju moved from Peak-of-the-gods to his house in the village. There, he wanted a field nearby where he could grow food. So he had hired some villagers to carve small terraces out of this hillside that he owned. The problem arose, however, because his old nemesis, the Witchdoctor, owned the adjoining land. The boundary between their two properties ran from a particular tree down the spine of a descending ridge. Over the years, Kalu had been moving the boundary stones to enlarge his holdings, but Baju had never complained. He was ten years older than Kalu, and he and the oldest people knew that the ridgeline was the ancient boundary. Consequently, he figured that he could reestablish that border if he ever needed to.

Most of the villagers were petrified of Kalu's witchcraft power, so they would never challenge him. Not so, Baju! Kalu himself was very thin, as was Baju when we first met him. But the longer Baju followed the Lord, the better his health became. The people told us that when a curse was put on them, they would become sick and get skinnier than ever. But Baju, they noticed, just got fatter and fatter with every curse.

A few days after the work started, Kalu discovered that Baju's new terraces were extending some ten or fifteen feet inside his boundary stones. This was his chance to register a case against Baju and have him fined. Even better, it would be the chance to bring public shame upon him. So Kalu hurried off to notify the village elders to come and see. Then he returned with his eldest son, and sat down on the barren hillside above a tiny goat trail.

Soon Baju came along, following the goat trail up from the spring. He was adept at getting around on his crutches, and though the trail was only the width of one's hand, he had no problem. His mind was on the terracing work, so he thought nothing of Kalu and his son perched there on the empty hillside.

Again and again, Kalu and his allies had been completely frustrated in their efforts to turn Baju back from following Jesus Christ. It seems that father and son must have been rehearsing their grudges against Baju, and finding him alone on the trail, their hatred erupted. Leaping upon him, they began to beat him with their fists. Their boiling rage, however, had befuddled their good sense, for they had forgotten about the elders... and at that very moment, two of them had just crested the knoll immediately behind them.

Before his leg had been blown off by a landmine on the Afghanistan border fifty-five years earlier, Baju would have been able to defend himself rather handily. But teetering now on two crutches on a six-inch wide trail, he was nearly helpless. Nevertheless, somehow Baju reached out with his left hand and caught hold of Kalu's shirt. Unleashing a powerful uppercut, his right fist crashed into Kalu's jaw, lifting the skinny old man off his feet and sending him tumbling down the mountainside into a thicket of briars.

Then, Baju grabbed the son's shirt and was in the act of a repeat performance when the elders arrived and stopped the fighting. Eventually, Kalu came crawling back up the steep slope on all fours and reached the goat trail scratched and bleeding. The elders, incredulous at witnessing an unprovoked attack, severely rebuked father and son.

That evening Baju came by to tell us the story. This was a serious crime in the village, and with the elders as eyewitnesses to the entire event, it was an open and shut case. Kalu and his son would be fined, but even worse, in front of the whole village they would be severely reprimanded and terribly shamed. Baju couldn't have dreamed of a finer opportunity to finally get revenge on his old adversary.

The next morning I was anxious to learn how it had turned out. Baju knew, however, how to treat one's enemies. He knew God's pattern in both the Old and New Testaments. God's way was to kill them with kindness. No, there had been no trial last night. Furthermore, he would not bring the accusation which everyone was expecting. Instead, he forgave and forgot. He knew how God expected him to treat his enemies. It was the same way that God had treated him. Whether it was King Solomon in Proverbs, or the Apostle Paul in the Book of Romans the command was the same:

> *"If your enemy is hungry, feed him;*
> *if he is thirsty, give him something to drink...*
> *Do not be overcome by evil, but overcome*
> *evil with good!"*
> Romans 12:20-21

—Postscript—

As for how he managed to defend himself on the goat trail, Baju had no idea. He supposed that the great strength that had suddenly surged through his body in those moments was the same power that God had given to King David when he killed the lion and the bear. He had no other explanation.

CHAPTER 37

VULTURES and ANGELS

Baju's interpretation of the scripture was so ridiculous that I could have fallen off my chair laughing if the ramifications hadn't been so serious.

I was doing a comprehension check on Chapter 17 of the Gospel of Luke. In a comprehension check, I would read a number of verses to Baju or one of the villagers, and ask him to tell me what it meant. If the explanation was off base, then we would rework the passage.

Figures of speech seldom transfer accurately across cultures, so when the scripture was figurative we always faced a special challenge. Time and again, we had initially translated such passages quite literally. But when I came to do the comprehension check, the villagers would come up with the most mind-boggling and heretical interpretations. Consequently, we would be forced to drop the figure of speech and replace it with a clear meaning.

For instance, let's suppose Luke had written, "King Herod had bought-the-farm." We would translate it, "King Herod died." We had to do that because the Magars would never guess that "bought-the-farm" figuratively meant that he had died. According to their language and idioms, they would say, "he fell." Or if he had died and been buried on the mountain, they might say, "he went to dig wild yams."

This time, however, the commentaries I relied on had ignored the verse altogether. Furthermore, I could not remember ever hearing a sermon that had dealt with it. So whether it would make sense to the Magars or not, we had translated it literally. Consequently, I had resigned myself to putting a lot of time into reworking it. Even before reading the verse I had said to Baju, "Well, you certainly won't be able to figure this one out!"

Then I read to him Luke 17:37 in Magar:

"Where, Lord?" they asked.

He replied, "Where there is a dead body, there the vultures will gather."

Baju's eyes closed to tiny slits and a great smile crept across his round bronze face, "Oh, that's easy!" he replied.

A bit taken back by his confident response, I braced myself for a theologically hair-curling application that had its genesis in the Magars' shamanistic and Hindu culture. After all, that was the only frame of reference that Baju knew.

"Well, of course," Baju began (which meant I surely must be joking or else I was really an ignorant dolt... something he would never actually voice):

214

"The meaning is that the angels will come and take us believers up to Heaven. The vultures are the angels and the dead bodies are us."

"Lord, have mercy," I thought. "Is this going to be another one of those obscure verses that is going to take us days and days to rework in order to make sense in Magar?"

Asking Baju how he came to that conclusion, he launched forth with enthusiasm:

"Well, first of all, vultures never die... or at least they live for a hundred years or more. No one knows whether they die or not because no one ever finds a dead vulture. Have you ever found a vulture's carcass? No! Maybe they die up in Tibet on the other side of the Himalayas or down in South India, but they don't die here. So, like the angels, they live forever."

"Secondly, vultures reside in the heavens. They soar so high that they are beyond the sight of man, yet we are not beyond their sight. Think about it: Just drag a dead cow or a dead dog out into a field some-time when there are no vultures to be seen in the sky. Within minutes, as if out of nowhere, vultures will be descending upon the carcass."

"Finally, what do vultures do? In consuming dead things they carry them back into the heavens."

"And as for us Believers... aren't we all supposed to be dead to this world? Aren't we to be unaffected by the lusts of the flesh, the pride of life, and the cares and worries of this world? Aren't we who trust in God supposed to be *dead* in Christ? Of course! If we are fully following Jesus, this world will have no more influence on us than it has upon a corpse!"

I was shocked. The idea of equating vultures with angels! It was really too much. But how could I fault him? Based on his world view, Baju's explanation fit the context perfectly.

Furthermore, I had no alternative to offer, so I decided to deal with it later. The problem was that I never came up with a better interpretation, and some twenty years later I am still waiting for an enlightened preacher to teach on that verse. Until then, a man from an ancient tribal culture, a completely unschooled, ignorant, and nearly illiterate villager in a dark corner of the Himalayas, has offered me a better explanation than the best theologians of the Western world.

> *"For you died, and your life is now hidden*
> *with Christ in God."*
> Colossians 3:3

CHAPTER 38

JERUSALEM

We were mentally exhausted and bone tired. We thought that three months in England would be more than sufficient for typesetting the Magar New Testament. Unexpected problems, however, had slowed our progress and day after day, week after week, Barbara and I had poured every last ounce of our energy into finishing.

Adina's wedding in Dallas was set for December 18, 1990, and we had to be there a month beforehand for Barbara to help with the arrangements. Our around-the-world tickets took us from London to Dallas and then back to Nepal. Thus, returning to England to finish up was not an option. Approaching completion, we were informed that there would be a two week delay to finalize the computer programming. I was exasperated. It was almost too much for me emotionally.

A couple of days later, however, we realized that this delay was from God. He was giving us an opportunity to take Baju to the Holy Land. On Monday, I phoned our Israeli friends who told us to come. On Tuesday, Baju and I made the trip into London to get his visa. At the Israeli Embassy, a large sign stated that a minimum of 24 hours was required to process **all** visa requests. I was feeling so tired, but I resigned myself to another train trip back into London. Without any explanation, however, the Israeli girl quietly asked us to sit down. Twenty minutes later she came out and slipped me Baju's passport with the visa.

On Wednesday, I purchased our plane tickets, and Thursday evening Moshe and Adina Keshet picked us up at the Tel Aviv airport. Our stay on their peaceful little farm in Bethlehem of Galilee (*see Joshua 19:15*) was greatly appreciated. Adina took us around and showed us the ancient fortress city of Meggido, which overlooked a spacious fertile valley known in scripture as Armaggedon.

From there we went to Tiberius to spend a night on the shore of Galilee. That evening, Barbara got to talking with a Finnish lady we had never met before. Elvi was distraught. She had been plagued by a problem for thirty long years. For months she had asked God to bring someone to help her during her upcoming trip to Israel. But God had **not** answered and she was flying back to Finland tomorrow. Barbara invited Elvi to our room and there, two hundred yards from the Sea of Galilee, she received her spiritual and emotional healing. The next morning, with a beaming face and overflowing praise to God, Elvi bid us goodbye.

In Jerusalem, we stayed on Mt. Zion. We were only a few hundred yards from King David's tomb, and about a ten-minute walk from the Temple Mount. Since the U.S. Consulate was nearby, I took this opportunity to stop in and apply for Baju's visa for the U.S. When our turn came, the lady at the window informed me that it was not possible for Third World nationals to get a visa outside their home country. She was so sorry, but her hands were tied. Baju would **not** represent the Magar people at Adina's wedding in December. Baju would have to return to Nepal.

I was stunned. I nearly cried. I wanted to tell her what an impossibility this was. Baju didn't speak English and he couldn't be expected to travel by himself. Furthermore, it was peak tourist season in Nepal and all the planes were booked up months ahead. There was no way to send him back.

I thought I had understood God's plan, but now it had all unraveled. I wish I could tell you that great faith rose up in my heart to conquer yet another crisis, but it just wasn't so. Instead, I stood there dumbfounded. The constant high level of stress required to complete the Magar New Testament had taken its toll. I had no reserves of energy left. I was emotionally beaten. I was mentally fatigued. Totally worn out.

Now I could no longer focus on God's plan. I didn't know what to pray. Defeated, dejected, and overcome, I turned away and trudged down the stairs with Baju. When I got back to our room on Mt. Zion I would have to rethink, pray, and discover God's plan all over again. However, just before we reached the last door, someone came running down the hall and told us to come back. The lady at the window said there was a long shot. She would ask her boss for special permission to fax Kathmandu... and at that very moment her boss walked by and gave his consent.

She urged me to phone any important people I knew in Kathmandu who could push through this special request. I could plan on getting an answer back within two weeks. But, unfortunately for me, all the people of importance that I had known were now gone. Furthermore, in only 48 hours the Consulate would close for the weekend, and on Sunday we were returning to England.

Friday morning came with the Consulate's noon-time closing deadline. I sat on our bed, barely able to lift my eyes to heaven, feeling perhaps like King Jehosaphat when he had prayed,

> *"We have no power to face this vast army*
> *that is attacking us. We do not know what to*
> *do, but our eyes are upon You."*
> 2 Chronicles 20:12

I tried to pray, I tried to meditate, I tried to focus on God... all with little success. I felt so weary. Hope and time seemed gone. As those last minutes passed, it felt like an executioner was closing in on me. Then at 10 a.m. the phone rang. "We have a fax from Kathmandu. Come quickly to collect Baju's visa!"

I hadn't felt at all sure that the visa would come, and I had prepared myself to somehow find a way to send Baju back to Nepal. Fortunately, God didn't seem bothered about how downcast I was feeling when I had prayed. Once more, on October 28, 1990, God came through.

—Postscript—

On Saturday, we took Baju up to the Mount of Olives. He was thrilled beyond words to have visited Israel and to have walked where his Savior had walked. To the East, we looked across the absolutely barren hills of Judea. Beyond them, perhaps fifteen miles away, we could see the Dead Sea clearly, and on the other side, the bone-dry mountains of Jordan. But turning around, in front of us now, lay the Garden of Gethsemane close below. Across a low little swale called Kidron and perhaps 200 yards further on was Jerusalem's Golden Gate. This gate is now closed, filled up with stone. But according to tradition, it will be opened for Messiah when He comes.

There on the Mount of Olives was the choice we always have: Look at the barrenness, the deadness, and the bitterness behind us, or look ahead to the hope and the promise to come!

—Barbara's Last Year—

(1991-1992)

CHAPTER 39

THE BIG FISH
❦❦❦

"Seek, and you will find.
Knock, and the door will be opened..."
Matthew 7:7

The huge fish exploded from the ocean depths. Then it tail-walked across the waves. What an incredible sight! I had practically been born with a fishing pole in my hand, but this sort of fishing was reserved for the rich... something I'd only seen in the movies or on TV.

Short though it was, it would be our last vacation together. For nearly two years, Barbara had been in good health and full of energy. But within three months, she would begin to fail again and we would lose her before the year had ended.

March of 1991 found Barbara and me in Malaysia. The Magar New Testament had been typeset in England and the negatives were being sent to the printer in Calcutta. (Later, we were to learn that they had been confiscated by customs officers in New Delhi.) Adina and Tom had gotten married in December and were living happily in Lubbock, Texas.

In those days, the most painful thing I faced was sending Michael far away to Boarding School in Penang. But there had been no alternative if we were to finish the Book. Time after time through the years, Adina and Michael had forfeited normal childhood opportunities so that we could continue our work. I was acutely aware of their sacrifices, and to compensate in some small way I always looked for something special to do with them. In this case, I thought to take Michael deep sea fishing. I knew that there were sailfish in the coastal waters of Malaysia and Thailand, but on our meager budget how would we ever manage an exotic trip like that?

The previous year, Barbara and I had been unable to get a resident visa in Nepal and had been stuck in Penang. Though we were there for ten weeks, I still hadn't managed to arrange even one small fishing trip. At Dalat School there were keen fishermen among the staff, but to my surprise, not one had ever tried for a sailfish. In January, however, my friend Ronnie Miller had given me a special $300 gift to help make it happen. So when I came across an advertisement for fishing in South Thailand, I sent a fax. I was pretty disappointed, however, when I received no response. In March, Michael's school had a long weekend off, so I decided to chance it anyway and gambled $285 on plane tickets to Phuket.

Walking the streets of downtown Phuket, we came across a fishing boat operator. They caught sailfish every week, or so their sales pitch went. I was rather dubious about this claim, but alternatives were few. When we set out the next morning, the sea was a little rough. After lunch, however, it settled down and we anchored over a deep ocean reef to jig for bait fish. While we were catching the small fish, something powerful took a bait that had been let down to the ocean floor. Michael pulled and reeled for a while and then I did, too. Grunting and straining, we eventually got the fish in close. After a number of misses, the boat hands finally slipped a noose around a 145 pound shark. With much thrashing, the fish was finally tied onto the back of the boat.

Soon, another large shark was hooked. This time, however, our line broke while he was right beside the boat! Almost immediately a school of sailfish surfaced about three hundred yards away. We pulled anchor and circled the feeding sailfish in order to draw a live bait into their midst.

Suddenly a huge fish erupted from the ocean. The reel screamed, the sailfish jumped. It did somersaults and tail-walked across the water in a most spectacular way. Finally, the sailfish was brought alongside. In attempting to boat it, however, the gaff bent in two and our sailfish fell back into the ocean!

I couldn't believe my eyes. After all this, were we to lose our trophy? A powerful fish like that is not easily boated. How long can one keep messing around without breaking the line or having the hook come loose? Straightening out their gaff handle, the boat hands tried again and amid a great deal of flailing, the fish was finally pulled over the gunwales. Michael had his trophy—a 7' 6" sailfish!

When we arrived back at the pier that evening, among the many fishing boats that had gone out, we were the only ones with big fish to hang up for show. Judging from the great jubilation of our crew, this was certainly not a weekly occurrence!

Realistically, it was hardly more than a far-fetched dream. However, we had kept on seeking and had ventured a substantial amount of money, and God had fulfilled the desires of my heart. To this day, Michael has this beautiful fish mounted on his wall. It reminds us of our last holiday with Barbara and of God's loving kindness to us who persistently seek.

—Postscript—

Baju was one who knew the Father's heart and he never seemed the slightest bit amazed when God answered prayer above and beyond our expectations. He would be delighted, of course, but not at all surprised when Michael caught a huge shark in addition to a big sailfish. His standard comment about such things was, "Ahh, God likes to give us extras."

Four months later, due to Barbara's failing health, we returned to Dallas for an indefinite stay.

Michael and Barbara with sailfish and shark

CHAPTER 40

A TROUBLED HEART

"Do not let your hearts be troubled.
Trust in God, trust also in Me."
John 14:1

That was the key. "Do not let!"
I had been letting my heart become troubled—
and the choice had been mine all along. It was so
obvious that morning. My focus was on the problem.
I had not been trusting in His promises to never leave
us. I had not been trusting in His promise to give us
a future and hope.

God had never spoken to me through His Word as
strongly as He did that day. I had used this Bible for
thirteen years and for the first time I recorded a date
in it... November 27, 1991. Then with a red pencil I
colored the words, *"Trust in God"* and drew a line to
that date.

The Magar New Testament had been printed and
successfully brought across the border. Now it was

being distributed. Six months earlier, Barbara had survived a massive mental breakdown while we were in Nepal. After coming out of the hospital, we had returned to Dallas and she was getting better, little by little. There were the usual ups and downs, but she was singing in the choir again and beginning to participate in things at the Wycliffe Center.

Out in San Diego, Barbara's mother was chronically bed-ridden. As an only child, Barbara felt responsible for her, and probably a little guilty. After all, since joining Wycliffe twenty-four years earlier, we had been gone most of the time, and her parents had hardly been able to enjoy their grandchildren. Although her father and their friends at church were quite able to look after things, Barbara needed to feel that she was available to help them whenever necessary. Consequently, we had been advised to remain in the U.S. for the last few years of her mother's life. Presently we were in Dallas to recover from the debilitating stresses which had accompanied the completion of the Magar New Testament. Once we had our strength back, we would need to take an assignment here at the Dallas center, so I wrote our Director in that regard.

When Barbara saw a copy of my letter discussing a potential reassignment, she became very distressed. We had been called by God to bring the Light to the Magar people! How could we turn back from *the call*? I tried to explain that we wouldn't be giving up on Nepal. After all, we could still go back at regular intervals for a few months at a time. She, however, needed to be available to help her mother. But for

Barbara, taking another assignment wasn't a satisfactory solution. It seemed to her like we were quitting.

Barbara's recovery had seemed to have reached a plateau. In order to move energetically into the future, I knew that we needed to regain our former strength. I had become overly burdened about this, and truly, I had let my heart be troubled.

This particular morning I had once again been asking God to bring a complete healing to Barbara. As I read this scripture, He spoke very clearly, *"Trust in God."*

"Yes," I thought, "Recovery is surely on the way."

As I rested upon Him afresh, my troubled heart was restored and renewed. Six days later, however, Barbara took her life.

It was probably another ten days before I had the emotional strength to go back and look at those words, *"Trust in God."* And there it was: The date that I had written in my Bible.

I still retained the peace of God, but it was all so confusing. I had been absolutely certain that she would recover, but instead she had tragically died. As I pondered it all, trying to grasp the words which had given me such hope and peace that day, I read Jesus' whole statement:

> *"Do not let your hearts be troubled.*
> *Trust in God, trust also in Me.*
>
> *In my Father's house are many rooms...*
> *And if I go and prepare a place for you*

I will come back and take you to be with Me
That you also may be where I am."
John 14:1-2

Now it all became clear. There was a healing, but not as I expected. The healing took place when Jesus had welcomed Barbara to that home He had been preparing for her.

JOHN 14:27

Nov 21, '91

Jesus Comforts His Disciples

14 "Do not let your hearts be troubled. Trust in God⁴; trust also in me. ²In my Father's house are many rooms; if it were not so, I would have told you. I am going there to prepare a place for you. ³And if I go and prepare a place for you, I will come back and take you to be with me that you also may be where I am. ⁴You know the way to the place where I am going."

My Bible—John 14:1-4

CHAPTER 41

ACKNOWLEDGE HIM

*"Trust in the Lord with all your heart,
and lean not on your own understanding."*
Proverbs 3:5

My mind was a jumble of confusion. I had found Barbara. She was gone. *Suicide.*

"Acknowledge Him!" The words were all but drowned out by the chaos in my mind. Again... gently... insistently, they pushed past the paralysis gripping me: *"Acknowledge Him!"* "Sounds like something from the Bible. There must be more to it," I thought.

Though it would take three or four days for me to recall the remainder of that well-loved Bible passage, nevertheless, for now that was enough. Somehow, someway I would trust Him. Now I couldn't think of what to do. I went outside and sat on the front doorstep with my head between my knees, my mind dazed and blank. I had to pull myself together. "Think!!!"

In a couple of minutes it came to me. "Yes, Joel, Steve, they will know!"

I went back inside and phoned my friends Steve VanRooy and Joel Warkentin. Again, I went out and sat down in the warm sun... numb and helpless. Joel, our colleague who lived across the street, arrived first. Steve had about the same distance to drive and he arrived a minute later. They rushed inside and after a bit came back out and said, "Gary, we have to call the police!"

Soon, sirens and horns were blaring as a police car and an ambulance came up our quiet street. I stood aside as people rushed in and out. Finally, a detective said he had to talk with me and very kindly he asked me to tell him all I knew.

*"Lean **not** on your own understanding."* For sure! How could I understand? How could I make sense out of it? For the next few days I went where friends took me and did what they told me to do. Of course there were decisions that were up to me, but I was surrounded by friends. That made the unbearable somehow bearable. When I was taken back to our home the next morning, distinctly I remember thinking, yes, even hoping, *"If only our car is stolen. If only our house is a pile of ashes, it would all be so fine. Without Barbara, they are meaningless!"*

Again and again during the week, the words *"acknowledge Him in all your ways"* would make their way through the turbulence that gripped my mind. To the best of my ability, I did. And He *did* direct my path.

A few days later, every vehicle traveling that six-lane road in Dallas came to a stop as the procession of over 50 cars made its way slowly to the cemetery. Some got out and stood beside their cars, some with hat in hand, even a few with a hand over their heart in honor of Barbara... for them, a person known only to God.

The emptiest times were still ahead, but they would not be empty of Him. And He, as promised, would direct my paths.

> *"In ALL your ways acknowledge Him,*
> *And He shall direct your paths."*
> Proverbs 3:6

—Postscript—

My mind was so shell-shocked that I have no memory of Tom Werkema who had come along with Steve. For some period of time he sat with me on the outside steps.

CHAPTER 42

I TRUST IN GOD

Why? Why couldn't it have been scheduled for yesterday? How could she possibly sing now? There were no guitars, no drums, no accompanying singers. Nothing to mask the slightest tremor in her voice. The recording, however, was now and this morning Adina was alone. It was her and God alone!

Some time back, Dr. Hines had picked out soloists for the annual album that the University A' Cappella Choir was to record. When he had assigned Adina the last verse of <u>My</u> <u>Father</u> <u>Watches</u> <u>Over</u> <u>Me</u>, no one would have guessed how real it would be for her on that day:

"The valley may be dark—the shadows deep.
But O', the Shepherd guards His lonely sheep.
And thru the gloom—He'll lead me home.
My Heavenly Father watches over me."

Countless times she had sung it flawlessly. That wasn't the problem. It was her emotions, her broken heart. How could she sing such words now without faltering? If she couldn't, Dr. Hines would understand. For this album, the full choir could sing it and no one would ever know. At Lubbock Christian University they talked of faith, they assumed faith, and they had sung of faith. But life was good, and generally the students didn't have a great need to put it to work. Today, however, they would know. Her choir friends would doubtless pray for Adina. But God? Today, would God show up?

The song had begun with the statement, *"I trust in God, I know He cares for me..."*

In the previous verse, her husband Tom's strong bass voice had just sung:

"He guides the eagle through the pathless air,
And surely, He remembers me..."

Would God remember her now? Adina came to the microphone as the choir was completing the refrain:

"I trust in God, I know He cares for me,
On mountain bleak, or on the stormy sea,
Though billows roll, He keeps my soul
My Heavenly Father watches over me."

Even though the semester's final tests were about to begin, as soon as this recording was finished, Adina was leaving school to come be with me. Only twelve hours earlier, Adina had been called out of her night class by the staggering news that her mother had committed suicide.

Dr. Hines had prophetically assigned her those words to sing, *"The valley may be dark—the shadows deep."* Could it be much deeper? Could it be much darker than now? But there was also the promise: *"The Shepherd guards His lonely sheep. And through the gloom, He'll lead me home—my Heavenly Father watches over me."*

Today, they would see if trusting God made any difference. Were these empty words or would God guard? Would He lead? Would He carry her over this dark chasm?

Today, it wouldn't be Prem, Darima, or Baju's faith, nor the faith of other Christians in Nepal whom she knew... people who had been persecuted, beaten, and jailed. Neither would it be the faith of her parents and friends. Today it would be her faith that was tested. Was it just religious teaching or had she learned to fellowship with Jesus? Were they just words or had a friendship with God become rooted deep within her heart?

As she came to the microphone, it was there and now it came forth in pure sweet melody. She could still trust in God! On the album she is just another good soloist for just another song. But for some, it was much, much more than that. It was a moment in time when the Good Shepherd truly guarded a lonely, devastated sheep. As He had promised, God proved Himself true to His promise for one who trusted.

*"..and the one who trusts in Him will never
be put to shame."*
Romans 9:33

CHAPTER 43

A TIME TO MOURN

"There is a time for everything...
a time to weep and a time to laugh,
a time to mourn and a time to dance."
Ecclesiastes 3:1, 4

On our way to the church for Barbara's funeral the Holy Spirit reminded me of Jesus' words, *"Blessed are those who mourn, for they shall be comforted,"* (Matthew 5:4).

I shared this with Adina and Michael, reminding them that Jesus didn't appear to offer any other alternative to mourning. It seemed that we had two choices: to mourn and be comforted, or to keep a stiff upper lip and rely on our self strength. We could pretend that we could manage okay, but in doing so we would choose not to receive God's comfort!

In one way we could claim that things were okay. Barbara was now released from those dark sieges of depression. And she wouldn't have to endure another psychotic episode when the wiring of her brain went awry and when her greatest fears became real live experiences. True, that was okay. But her death was not okay. It was not okay for Adina and Michael to have lost their mother at the age of forty-nine. The truth was that each of us would miss her terribly. It was something to be deeply sad about.

But God had a way to bring us through. He had a plan that would bless us, if we remained open to His ways. Or... we could do it our own way. We could hide our pain, put on a good front, and hope that time would heal us. Relying on time, however, was trusting in a false hope. Feverish activity might distract one's mind, and time might put it at a distance and obscure the pain. But in reality, its effects would hound us forever. True healing, Jesus said, would come by mourning.

I didn't like it, but I accepted it, and I determined that I would do it God's way. I would trust Him to apply His healing medicine to my soul. No matter how much it hurt, I would enter in... because Jesus had promised that if I did so, I would ultimately be comforted. God didn't say how long it would take, but for sure comfort would come and be the antidote for my pain.

In May 1992, five months later, I found myself in Kathmandu. I had arranged to stay with Mick and Mary Haegeland, but when I arrived they were in the throes of moving to Pokhara. I would have to find someplace else. Mick did say that our old home had come empty, and I could stay the night there if I wanted. I didn't want to, but after traveling half way around the world, I didn't have the energy to look for other options that afternoon.

Mick was so very sorry. Others had been staying in our old house and their own move to Pokhara had come about suddenly. He offered to find someplace else for me. But when I walked in the front door I knew instantly that God had arranged it all. I understood. My time had come.

We had first rented this house fifteen years earlier, in February 1977. Adina would have been five and Michael three. For many years this home had been the center of the happiest days of our lives. Baju had often lived here with us, sometimes for two or three months at a time. Many from the village had come and stayed here while their family members had medical treatment or operations. Much of our translation work had been accomplished in this house, but now everything had changed. The renters had moved out leaving it stripped and barren. In a corner of our bedroom was a rickety old bed that had been left behind. Beside it there was a shaky bed stand where I placed my cassette player.

In the daytime, I went around Kathmandu visiting friends, and researching how to build a road into Arakhala. In the evenings I would come back to this dark, empty, dilapidated house and climb into bed. Every night I followed the same routine: insert my favorite praise music and play through the songs until I fell asleep.

Those words of praise reiterated how happy and fulfilling life was when one walked with the Lord and was obedient. But that house and that room in particular presented such a stark contrast. It made the words of those songs seem like a lie. All the laughter, all the joy of the kids growing up... it was now all gone. In front of me was a single light bulb dangling from a wire in the ceiling. Paint was blistering and pealing on the cement walls. Remnants of curtains were hanging on the windows, and light bulbs were burnt out or missing.

I was a widower now, and the only blessing I seemed to have left was those old memories. I was alone in a once-happy house... a house now empty of furniture, empty of pictures, empty of laughter, and empty of family. Through the years we had proved true those songs of promise and blessing, but today those words appeared dreadfully false. I was so alone. I was so very sad!

Then, there were choruses such as the one from the Book of Job:

> *"You give and take away;*
> *You give and take away;*
>
> *My heart will choose to say;*
> *Blessed be the Name of the Lord."*

Without a doubt, this was my destiny. Hot tears streamed down my face at the emptiness I felt. When a chorus such as this ended, I would back up the tape and listen to it again and again... and yet again. When my pain had exhausted all the tears, I turned off the player and fell asleep. In the morning I would turn the tape back on. When another song cut deeply into my heart, I would play it again and again... until there were no more tears. For ten days I was relentless and ruthless... until finally, neither pain nor tears could be found.

I knew then that I had completed the bulk of the therapy. I had done it in God's place, in God's way, and in God's time. I had wept for the past. I had wept for the present. I had faced the cold hard truth: The truth that I was alone, simply alone. Me and God alone. My vivacious and dedicated wife was gone, never to return. I didn't like it, but I accepted that fact. Life had a huge empty hole in it, and it would never be the same again. But now it would be okay... just me and God, alone.

In the coming months it was assumed by some that the peace and happiness I exhibited was a cover-up for my loss. They thought, so it was said, that my life would unravel one day and I would have an emotional meltdown. But they didn't ask, so I didn't tell... of those ten days when I chose. When I chose God and sang through the tears, *"You give and take away."* When I chose to trust Jesus' promise that God would comfort me.

> *"Blessed are those who mourn, for they* ***shall*** *be comforted."*
> Matthew 5:4

CHAPTER 44

THE DREAM

✿✿✿

For about a hundred hours after Barbara died, I experienced a deep anguish. The singing at Barbara's funeral soothed the worst of that pain, and the next day in church it was reduced further when folks prayed for our family. But even after this initial round of tears, there still remained a great heaviness in my heart.

Three weeks later, when friends greeted me with *"Merry Christmas,"* I felt even worse. They had meant well, but how could life be *merry* for me! After Christmas, Ben and Paulette Boothe invited Michael and me to go skiing with them in New Mexico. We greatly appreciated this offer. The mountains and snow-laden trees were beautiful and a real change from Dallas. We skied and sledded and had a fun time with the Boothe family.

Then on December 31st, Michael and I started the long drive back to Dallas. This day would have been our 26th wedding anniversary and I had been dreading that it would feel as sad and lonely as Christmas had felt. As we passed through the empty range lands of West Texas, I began to recall a short dream I had had early that morning.

This was the first time in months that I could remember dreaming. The dream was of Barbara and me together at the front of a little church. As I mulled it over and over in my mind the symbolism slowly emerged. God was reminding me:

"On this day 26 years ago, Barbara's father gave her to you. And you took it upon yourself to care for, comfort, and love her. Now, however, she is with Me. I am caring for her; I am comforting her and giving her all the love she needs."

Barbara was a gift from Father God and in a place of worship, Barbara's father had given her to me. If her father hadn't willingly given her away, we would have eloped and there would have been no blessing for him. But now, it was my turn. The message was clear: I needed to give her back to her Father in heaven.

It was four weeks to the day since Barbara had left me. As God spoke to my heart through this dream, I was able to willingly give her back to Him. I had already done that with my mind, but I had continued to hold onto her in my heart. We were now into the last hours of 1991, and God wanted me to close out the old year emotionally whole. Just as it had been Barbara's father's choice, now it was my choice.

I could have deceived myself and pretended that she was still mine, but I didn't. God had asked and I responded. After I had given her to our Father, I discovered that He began to slowly fill that chasm of emptiness where I had held Barbara. For the first time since she had left me, I was able to rejoice over her in my heart.

My best efforts hadn't been enough to keep her safe, but now she was safe forever with the Father and I could be glad. Around the world, countless people had prayed for me. God had heard and answered on just the right day. Our Sunday School teacher, Angie Hammond, had said to me, "Time will never heal you, but God will, in His time."

Her loving advice was now being fulfilled. By Sunday, a degree of normality had returned in my heart and I was able to sing every song in the worship service. That great emptiness felt like it had been filled. The wound seemed all healed. I soon discovered, however, that this was just the beginning. Day after day, for many, many months to come, God would continue to tangibly fill that emptiness with more and more of Himself.

Before long, I would be taking Michael back to Malaysia for his last semester of high school and then proceed on to Nepal. Now, instead of going back overseas full of sadness and in weakness, I was returning with a degree of strength and with rejoicing. Who could believe such a wonderful change could happen so soon? I could only repeat, *"The Lord has done great things for us, and we are filled with joy* (Psalm 126:3)."

Throughout this ordeal I was determined to thank God for every blessing He brought my way. From then on, I refused to allow my focus to dwell for long on what I had lost. I didn't realize it, but in thanking Him for what I did have, I was preparing a pathway for God to bless me. King David refers to this when he wrote, *"He who sacrifices thank offerings honors Me, and he prepares the way so that I may show him the salvation of God,* (Psalm 50:23).*"*

To my amazement, my thanks would do more than prepare the way for God. In addition, He counted my thanks as an honor to His Name!

There would be other times of weeping and sorrow. In May, there would be ten days of weeping in Kathmandu. The tears, however, would no longer be for Barbara, but rather for me and my aloneness. My response to the dream had lifted the responsibility for Barbara off my shoulders. Now I fully understood Who was looking out for her.

As for the bottomless hole in my heart, week after week He kept pouring His love into that empty chasm. If I had attempted to keep her locked away in my heart, I would have only deceived myself and denied God access to the path that would restore me with His Presence and love!

"The Lord gave, and the Lord has taken away;
Blessed be the Name of the Lord."
Job1:21

CHAPTER 45

Suicide is a subject often avoided in our culture. This article gives some insight into the family background and dynamics as well as the stresses of living in Nepal which contributed to Barbara's mental breakdown and subsequent suicide. My prayer is that something here will be helpful to others who have been touched by suicide.

THE SACRIFICE

Barbara Shepherd
(November 5, 1942 - December 3, 1991)

B arbara's parents grew up near Salina, Kansas, during the Great Depression. Her father, Hamilton, was the oldest of six. In order to help support a family struggling without a father, he left school at age fourteen. As a teenager, he excelled in boxing, becoming the Golden Gloves Champion of

Kansas State. However, he had no money for travel, so he missed his opportunity to compete for the U.S. national boxing title.

Barbara's mother, Lucille, remembered the Great Drought at that time, which ruined the farmers. Many of them could not pay their bills at her father's little store. Consequently, Lucille's family was poor also—so poor that she had only one dress to wear in high school. She often commented on how this made her feel very ashamed.

After Ham and Lucille were married, they left the drought-stricken land and drove out to San Diego, California, where Ham found a job as a welder. Later, he worked twelve hours a day as a riveter, building B-17 bombers for the war effort. Living nearby was Mae Malone, a jolly, likeable, divorced lady. She had been an attractive southern belle, enjoying the high society life. However, at the age of forty, she asked Jesus to become the Lord of her life, and subsequently her husband had divorced her. Childless and without other ties, Mae passionately invested her considerable energy and skills into improving the lives of others.

Ham and Lucille were frugal and hard working. Barbara was their only child and she was particularly bright and gifted with considerable musical abilities. Among other things, she was featured playing the piano on a local radio station at the age of five. When she was eight, Mae Malone invited her to her back-yard Bible class where Barbara committed her heart to the Lord. In the following years, dear Mae missed no opportunity to keep Barbara involved in numerous church youth events in the San Diego area.

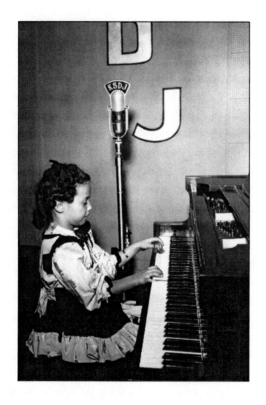

Barbara at the radio station

In high school, Barbara participated in a multitude of activities including a dance band in which she played the saxophone. When Mae saw the ways of the world pulling ever stronger, she encouraged Barbara to graduate early from high school. So at age sixteen, Barbara entered Simpson Bible College where she excelled in all subjects. In addition to becoming the Senior Queen, she graduated at the top of her class. Along the way, she felt God's call to offer her life for missions and was accepted to serve overseas as a school teacher with the Christian & Missionary Alliance.

When she took a fifth year of studies in education at San Diego State University, she again graduated at the top of her class. Just before finishing, she met me at a home Bible study associated with the College Avenue Baptist Church. Five months earlier, I, a one time blasphemer, sinner, and enemy of God, had by His grace and mercy, set my heart to following in the way of Jesus. As a junior officer in the U.S. Navy and just an average guy, it seemed incredible that she should take any interest in me.

Whether playing the piano or organ, directing the Sunday School program or leading the choir, Barbara always excelled. She claimed that she was an *over-achiever*. She surpassed others who were smarter by working harder and studying longer.

She always felt a deep responsibility to make her life count for God's Kingdom, and she couldn't say *no* to a request. As a result, she regularly took on too much. Ten months after we were married, she collapsed on our stairs one day and began to weep. She had become the best first grade teacher in her school, as well as the best of everything else. She was simply exhausted from trying to fulfill all of the demands she put on herself. It seemed to be her nature to willingly sacrifice herself for others.

A few months after we were married, she was a bit surprised when I wanted to join Wycliffe Bible Translators. However, after we took the first linguistics course, in which she excelled, we became members in 1967. In Nepal, she did very well at learning the languages, though she was always concerned that she wasn't doing better.

When Adina was born, Barbara couldn't devote the same effort to the Magar language project as she had before. So we decided that she would take over the village medical work which I was doing, and I would devote more of my time to the language analysis. Her deep compassion and care made her particularly effective at working with the sick. The negative side, however, was that she would feel overly responsible when people became seriously ill.

Teaching Adina reading in the village

257

In those days, our life alternated between living in Kathmandu and Arakhala Village. When the children reached school age, Barbara taught them during the time we were in the village. In the following years, she became increasingly concerned if they didn't score near the top of their classes in Kathmandu. As we approached the end of each school year, it became more and more stressful for her.

When Adina got average grades in English in the 4th grade, Barbara became quite distressed. Surely Adina was going to fail and it would be her fault! I pointed out that Adina had become simultaneously fluent in Magar, Nepali, and English. My assessment of Adina's strong language skills, however, gave Barbara no solace. What kind of mother would she be if Adina failed 4th grade?

Rumors abounded in those days that the Chinese Army, on their way into India, would attack Nepal without warning and swallow us up overnight. Additionally, there was the constant stress of Nepali Christian friends and acquaintances being threatened, beaten, and put into jail. Also, our mail was regularly intercepted and read by government intelligence agents. In 1976, our project was shut down and we were forced to leave the country. Six months later, however, Barbara and I returned so that we could continue to work with the Magar people. All the time, however, there was an underlying fear that our translation work would be found out and we be expelled for good.

These and other stresses resulted in system overload, and at the end of 1982, Barbara had a psychotic episode. Returning to the village, we had just begun to ascend the steep mountain range when we passed a villager listening to his transistor radio. Barbara turned to me and with a knowing smile, asked if I had heard the news. I hadn't, so she filled me in. "The police are sending out a detachment to arrest the Shepherds because of their Christian work!"

I explained to her that this couldn't be right. The police didn't broadcast their intents before apprehending criminals. I assumed that she had simply misheard; I didn't realize that this was a psychotic episode. Later, Dr. David Stengel, our friend who had worked in Nepal, explained how this can happen: Excessive stress and constant fear deplete the neurotransmitter chemicals in the brain. (For some people, unforgiveness and the accompanying suppressed anger can do this, too.) If the chemical level gets too low, the brain's thoughts begin to slip off their proper routing. It's almost like a telephone line in Nepal when the telephone wire has a loose connection or its insulation covering has rubbed off. Then it shorts out to a nearby line and we hear a second conversation.

If one has a deep-seated fear, the continued rerunning of that fear in one's mind can be like tires digging deep ruts into a muddy road. Later, when the next vehicle comes along it may slip into those ruts and be unable to extract itself for some distance. Fears of being expelled by the authorities had dug deeply into her mind. When the chemical levels had gotten out of balance, her thoughts had slipped off their proper routing and had begun to connect up haphazardly.

Fortunately, this sort of thing did not continue for long. Usually, a night's rest would restore her, and all would be normal again the next day... except that this fearful *experience* had now become a part of her memories.

After one of those episodes, something intangible changed. In some respects it was like she had had a mini-stroke. No one ever mentioned it to me, but I could see. Though she always tried hard, she never again had quite the same brightness in her smile. Also, her vivacious spirit and whole-hearted laughter were somehow tempered. Meanwhile, Barbara had begun to experience times of depression. At first, it seemed that the depression might last for a day or two, and then she would carry on as before. Her condition would cycle, and most of the time she was quite well. Early on, I did not understand and assumed that she was just having a bad day or a bad week.

Barbara had deep compassion for others in distress and would go to great lengths to consol, pray for, or help them. She could be counted on for a listening ear or to offer a shoulder to cry on. Though she would listen to others' deepest pain, she was usually unable to share her own burdens, even with me. And when I wanted to ask friends to pray for her at times, she could become very upset with me and say that I was telling family secrets!

Later on, her own mother became deeply depressed, eventually lying in bed for seven years. Lucille usually resisted the doctors' advice or what the family tried to do to help her. She would insist that she did not need help. She was just fine!

While we were in Nepal finishing the last parts of the Magar New Testament, we went to a lot of expense for Barbara to phone home regularly. Each time, her mother asked when we were coming back. When she realized we wouldn't be back for a couple of years, she tried a different tactic. In subsequent phone calls, her weak voice became interspersed with croaking coughs, and it sounded as if she were not far from death. Alarmed at first, we phoned Adina and asked about Grandmother. However, when Adina reported that Grandma always sounded just fine when she talked with her, it became clear that she was trying to manipulate us to return to the U.S.

Nevertheless, Barbara eventually became convinced that her mother was dying and she, her only child, was not there to help! After returning from Calcutta to check the New Testament plates at the printers in May of 1991, Barbara slipped into a massive mental breakdown. Her fears had developed into reality for her: Her mother was dying in the hospital! Her mother was dead! A close friend was about to be assassinated! Chinese helicopters were coming to capture Michael and carry him away!

It took six weeks before Barbara was settled sufficiently to board a plane and return to the U.S. There, Dr. Stengel admitted her to a hospital in Idaho and got her stabilized. He counseled me that eventually we could probably live in Nepal again, but because of her mother's controlling influence, it would be not until she had passed away.

In August we arrived at our home in Dallas and Barbara slowly got back into a routine. A couple of times, she told me that she could never go through a mental breakdown again. It was so dreadfully dark, she said, like living in hell! In October, I wrote our Director to tell him that we needed to be reassigned until Barbara's mother passed away, which in any case didn't seem too far away. Meanwhile, Barbara had begun singing again in the church choir and was attending a seminar at the Wycliffe Center.

Unfortunately, about a month later, Barbara came across a copy of my letter to our Director, and it became obvious that she could not face the idea of delaying our return to Nepal. About a month after the dedication of the Magar New Testament in Dallas, she thought of a way to continue our work with the Magars. She was the problem. She was keeping me from going back to the village. As she had done all her life, once again she would sacrifice herself. This time, it seems, for me and the Magars.

On December 3rd, she had her own plan, which she had hidden from me and friends, as well as her doctor, whom she had seen the previous day. That morning she dressed herself particularly well and gave me an extra-long hug. I was unsuspecting. While she was writing Christmas cards, I went over to the Wycliffe Center to get a small computer problem fixed. When I returned, I found her dead.

Barbara had never made any mention of suicide. A week earlier she had even assured Adina that, of course, she would never do that! There was no note. The only clue she left us was a clothes hanger laid upon her open Bible. The top of the page began with Romans 12:1:

"Therefore, I urge you, brothers, in view of God's mercy, to offer your bodies as living sacrifices..."

Though Romans refers to a *living sacrifice*, her mind had failed to compute the *living* part. Since one's will and personality are expressed via the physical brain, to separate its bona fide failure from an act of the will can be difficult. I know I cannot *will* my old clouded eye to see better, or *will* my worn out ears to hear more clearly. Still, when the brain is getting cross-wired, it is hard to understand why one cannot just pull it all together. These illusions, however, were vivid, real life experiences for her. They became imprinted in her memory and were never forgotten.

I have learned that if I do not eat extra calcium on our exhausting treks, I will get leg cramps. I know that insufficient water in my car's radiator will cause the engine to seize up. But an imbalance of chemicals in one's brain, resulting in the misrouting of information... that seems somehow different. However, it really is not. And when one acts upon that misinformation, as Barbara did... it can result in a tragic ending.

Though she strived to be perfect in her service to the Lord, it is only now that she has been made perfect. Ultimately, our only sure hope is that we will live with Him in heaven because of His great love and His sacrifice... not ours.

"There is therefore now no condemnation for those who are in Christ Jesus..."
Romans 8:1

CHAPTER 46

ALL COMFORT

❧ ❦ ❧

How could I do it? Would God's comfort be sufficient? Would His peace be greater than the pain? If I were to offer comfort to the hurting, I could not avoid revisiting my own deepest sorrows. For sure, there would be no easy way.

The dream came just four weeks later, on our 26th wedding anniversary. Meditating on the meaning of the dream, where Barbara and I stood at the front of a small church, God led me to give her over to Him just as her own father had given her to me 26 years earlier. Doing that released my heart from the burden of responsibility I had felt for her. As a result, my shattered heart was set free and the God of all comfort began to occupy that emptiness.

A couple of weeks later, I took Michael back for his last semester of high school at Dalat Boarding School in Malaysia. From there, I went on to Nepal where I sought out many of our long-time friends. The degree of comfort I was experiencing so soon after this tragedy was unusual. I realized then that God would have me share it just as Paul had written,

"Praise be to God...the God of all comfort,
who comforts us in all our troubles, so that
we can comfort those in any trouble with the
comfort we ourselves have received from God."
2 Corinthians 1:3-4

The responsibility to share what I had received was clear. I knew, however, that whenever I shared this comfort I would also relive my loss. But that was clearly the Master's way... sacrificing oneself that others might become free. After seeing our friends in Nepal, I traveled around the U.S. to visit those people who had been Barbara's old friends. I would share with them Barbara's ten-year struggle with depression and the episodes of psychosis when the wires in her brain got crossed.

I would tell them of the time I found Barbara in an empty room at midnight turning a light switch on and off, explaining that, "The Communists are coming to get us! I'm signaling the police for help!" I had convinced her that all was well and she had gone back to bed. The night's rest had replenished the chemical balance in her brain and the next day she seemed fine.

Her friends wept over the struggles and trials that Barbara had encountered, and all the more so as she had soldiered on to see the Magar New Testament completed. I comforted them with the comfort I had received through the dream, through scripture, through friends, and through God's many special kindnesses to me.

When I told of her suicide, many of her friends were dumbfounded. About a third of them, however, shared then of their own experiences with suicide... an uncle, a grandparent, or a brother. For most, this had been a well-kept family secret and its pain had been chained to the bottom of their hearts. "You are the first one we have told," they sometimes confided. Again there was more weeping and more comforting.

One of my favorite verses had always been Jesus' words, *"You will know the truth and the truth will set you free,"* (John 8:32).

I encouraged them to hide the truth no longer. Revealing the truth would go far in setting them free from the agony and sadness their tragedy was producing. It would require them to face the pain and mourn, but Jesus had promised that those who mourned would also be comforted! (Matthew 5:4)

Back in January, Paul and Norma Seefeldt had told me that I didn't have to be alone, and that I should drop by their house at any time. When I was in Kathmandu at the end of October, I stopped by one day to find Norma at home. As we talked, I noticed the picture of a man on her refrigerator and asked about him. A heart-breaking story emerged.

Three months earlier, on July 31, 1992, a large jet had slammed into the mountains near Kathmandu. Thirty days later, another jet crashed the same way! Among the dead on each plane was a missionary family returning to Nepal. The picture on the refrigerator was the father of one of those families. They were close friends of the Seefeldts. Recognizing Norma's pain, I shared the many ways in which God had brought me comfort. Then I prayed for her. Afterwards, she told me how much my sharing had helped. She mentioned then that she had friends who were hurting even more than her, so I offered to share with them also.

Two days later, I was back at Norma's for dinner to share this comfort with Kirk and Paula Dunham. Norma was a nurse and during the evening the name of another missionary nurse came up. My mind, however, was focused on bringing them God's comfort, and anyways, I had never heard of this person. Later, as Paula and Norma took care of the dishes, I was drinking coffee and talking more with Kirk. Standing in the kitchen, the revelation came to both of them at the same time, *"Kerry!"* Norma marched straight out to me and declared, "You need to meet Kerry Brown! She's the perfect match for you!"

The next day I did and she was! Because I had been willing to relive my pain again and again and again... and share the comfort of God, I came to Norma and Paul's house that evening. It was God's plan... the way He would provide me with even more comfort and joy. In fact, her middle name was Joy—Kerry Joy Brown! It will take another whole book, however, to tell you all the stories of our joys and adventures together with the Magars of Nepal.

(To be continued in Part II with "That Nurse.")

Breinigsville, PA USA
26 October 2009

226513BV00001B/2/P